FROM GUNPOWDER TO GUNS

First published in 2009 by Middlesex University Press

ISBN 978 1 904750 85 7

A CIP catalogue record for this book is available from The British Library

Design by Helen Taylor

Maps by Alice Gadney of Silver7 Mapping Ltd

Printed in the UK by Ashford Colour Press

Middlesex University Press
The Burroughs
Hendon
London NW4 4BT

Tel: +44 (0)20 8411 4162
Fax: +44 (0)20 8411 4167

www.mupress.co.uk

FROM GUNPOWDER TO GUNS

the story of two Lea Valley armouries

Jim Lewis

Middlesex University
PRESS

The RSA Factory today (2009)

RSA Trust

The RSA Trust The RSA Island Centre, Enfield Island Village,
33 Island Centre Way, Enfield Middlesex EN3 6GS

Dear Reader

It was with great pleasure that I accepted the opportunity to write a few words to preface this book.

The word 'regeneration' is regularly used by modern-day planners and developers when describing major changes to a site, area or region. However, it is not always possible to regenerate satisfactorily all run-down industrial areas, particularly if the communities that supported them grew up around an industry based on a single commodity.

The Royal Small Arms Factory had sustained the local community with both employment and a range of supporting facilities for over 170 years. When closure was announced in 1987, few believed that regeneration of any sort was possible. Fortunately, the factory had its roots in the Lea Valley which for centuries had supported many diverse industries; and when one declined, another, perhaps quite different, took its place.

When plans were made to build over 1,300 new homes on the site, a group of local businessmen came together in 1995 to see what they could do to bring back into use the Grade II listed machine shop of the Royal Small Arms Factory. They gave freely of their time to establish RSA Island Village Limited, a not-for-profit-company whose vision was to transform the machine shop into the village centre for the new community and run it on a strictly commercially viable basis that would benefit the local community, while retaining the historic spirit of the place and its iconic clock tower.

In 2004, they set up the RSA Trust, a registered charity which supports regional 'good cause' projects through revenue generated by the village centre. To date, the RSA Trust has distributed approaching £2m, including support for youngsters on the Island and local businesses. Thus the former factory site, with the old machine shop as its hub, has once more become the heart of a vibrant local community. The unique village centre provides residents with a health centre and pharmacy, childcare facilities, library, youth centre, fitness facility, shops, food outlets and a community hall. An example of a sensitive and successful regeneration project, this thriving new community is clearly looking forward to a bright future.

The RSA Trust is very pleased to support Jim Lewis's book, which enables readers to see both what the RSA factory looks like today and how it looked in times gone by.

Gary Walker
Chairman, the RSA Trust
www.rsatrust.org
June 2009

DEDICATION

This book is dedicated to my family and also to my late mother and father, Leonora Maud Lewis and Walter Harry Portman Lewis.

ABOUT THE AUTHOR

Dr Jim Lewis has spent most of his career in the consumer electronics industry, apart from a three-year spell in the Royal Air Force servicing airborne and ground wireless communications equipment. When working in the Lea Valley for Thorn EMI Ferguson he represented the company abroad on several occasions and was involved in the exchange of manufacturing technology. Currently he is a Consultant to Terry Farrell & Partners on the historical development of London's Lea Valley and a Workers' Educational Association (WEA) tutor teaching industrial history. He also teaches students within the Community Programme who have learning difficulties. A freelance writer, researcher and broadcaster for his specialist subject - London's Lea Valley - he also has a genuine passion for encouraging partnership projects within the local community, which in the long term are planned to help stimulate social and economic regeneration. Dr Lewis is married with four grown-up children and lives in Lincolnshire.

The author Dr Jim Lewis cutting the ribbon, with the Director of the Pump House Steam & Transport Museum Trust, Lindsay Collier MA, to open a special exhibition commemorating the 90th anniversary of the birth of the Associated Equipment Company (AEC), Walthamstow, the company responsible for the founding of London Transport (now Transport for London). Lindsay Collier and the Pump House Steam & Transport Museum Trust are responsible for designing and promoting the *Lea Valley Experience* project.

SERIES ACKNOWLEDGEMENTS

The author wishes to thank the following organisations, companies and societies for their encouragement, support and advice and for supplying many of the illustrations within this book:

Alexandra Palace and Park Trust, Wood Green, London
BAE Systems, Farnborough, Hampshire
Bishopsgate Institute, London
Black & Ethnic Minority Business Association, Walthamstow, London
BOC Process Plants, Edmonton, London
Brooklands Museum, Weybridge, Surrey
Bruce Castle Museum, Tottenham, London
Civix, Exton Street, London
Corporation of Trinity House, Tower Hill, London
Cuffley Industrial Heritage Society, Cuffley, Hertfordshire
Edmonton Hundred Historical Society, Enfield, Middlesex
Enfield Archaeological Society, Enfield, Middlesex
Enfield Business Centre, Enfield, Middlesex
Enfield Energy Centre Limited, Enfield, Middlesex
Enfield Enterprise Agency, Enfield, Middlesex
Enfield Local History Unit, Enfield, Middlesex
English Heritage, Blandford Street, London
Epping Forest Museum, Waltham Abbey, Essex
Greater London Record Office, Northampton Road, London
Gunpowder Mills Study Group, Guildford, Surrey
Guy & Wright Ltd., Green Tye, Hertfordshire
Hackney Society, Hackney, London
Harper Collins Publishers, Hammersmith, London
Hawker Siddeley Power Transformers, Walthamstow, London
Historical Publications Ltd., Barnsbury, London
Hornsey Historical Society, Hornsey, London
House of Lords Record Office, Westminster, London
Imperial War Museum, Duxford, Cambridgeshire
Institution of Civil Engineers, George Street, London
Institution of Engineering and Technology, Savoy Place, London
Institution of Mechanical Engineers, Birdcage Walk, London
Jewish Museum, Finchley, London
John Higgs, Freelance Historian, Fairford, Gloucestershire
Johnson Matthey, Enfield, Middlesex
Lea Valley Growers Association, Cheshunt, Hertfordshire
Lee Valley Business and Innovation Centre, Enfield, Middlesex
Lee Valley Regional Park Authority, Enfield, Middlesex
London Borough of Enfield, Enfield, Middlesex
London Borough of Haringey, Haringey, London
London Borough of Newham, East Ham, London
London Borough of Waltham Forest, Walthamstow, London
London Lee Valley Partnership Limited, Great Eastern Street, London
London Organising Committee of the Olympic & Paralympic Games, Canary Wharf, London
LondonWaste Ltd, Edmonton, London
Lotus Engineering, Hethel, Norwich, Norfolk
Marconi Archive, Oxford University Library Services, Oxford, Oxfordshire

Markfield Beam Engine & Museum, Tottenham, London
Midland Publishing Limited, Earl Shilton, Leicester
Ministry of Defence Library, Royal Armouries, Leeds, Yorkshire
Museum of London, London Wall, London
National Archive, Kew, Richmond, Surrey
National Army Museum, Chelsea, London
National Maritime Museum, Greenwich, London
National Portrait Gallery, London
Natural History Museum, Kensington, London
Navtech Systems Ltd., Market Harborough, Leicestershire
New River Action Group, Hornsey, London
Newham Local History Library, Stratford, London
North London Strategic Alliance, Wood Green, London
Perkins Group, Leyton, London
Phillips Auctioneers & Valuers, New Bond Street, London
Potters Bar Historical Society, Potters Bar, Hertfordshire
Pump House Steam & Transport Museum, Walthamstow, London
RCHME Cambridge, (National Monuments Record), Cambridge, Cambridgeshire
Reuters Limited, Fleet Street, London
River Lea Tidal Mill Trust, Bromley-by-Bow, London
Royal Air Force Museum, Hendon, London
Royal Commission on Historic Manuscripts, Quality Court, Chancery Lane, London
Royal Society of Chemistry, Burlington House, London
Royal Television Society, Holborn Hall, London
Science Museum, Kensington, London
Scout Association, Chingford, Essex
Southgate District Civic Trust, Southgate, London
Speedway Museum, Broxbourne, Hertfordshire
Stratford City Challenge, Stratford, London
Tesco, Cheshunt, Hertfordshire
Thames Water, Reading, Berkshire
Thorn EMI Archive, Hayes, Middlesex
Tower Hamlets Local History Library, Tower Hamlets, London
University of Leicester Space Research Group, Leicester, Leicestershire
Upper Lee Valley Partnership, Tottenham Hale, London
Valley Grown Nurseries, Nazeing, Essex
Vauxhall Heritage, Luton, Bedfordshire
Eric Verdon-Roe, grandson of Alliott Verdon-Roe
Vestry House Museum, Walthamstow, London
Waltham Abbey Royal Gunpowder Mills Company Ltd., Waltham Abbey, Essex
Walthamstow Amateur Cine Video Club, Walthamstow, London
WEA, London District, Luke Street, London
Wordsworth Editions, Ware, Hertfordshire

While many individuals have freely given their knowledge, some unknowingly, which has contributed greatly to the production of this series of books, I have, on a number of occasions paid special tribute to certain people in the footnotes of various chapters.

I could not let the occasion pass without recording my sincere thanks to my wife Jenny for her superb editorial skills and outstanding patience. The author freely admits that this voluntary sacrifice on Jenny's part has comprehensively tested the cement that holds our wonderful marriage together.

AUTHOR'S NOTE

Events such as the Olympics can be brought into our homes and workplaces from the host country as they take place through the power of electronic communication - radio, television, the Internet and satellite broadcasts. The technology that allowed this to happen was first discovered and developed at Ponders End, Enfield in London's Lea Valley.

In November 1904, after much experiment, Professor Ambrose Fleming registered his patent for the diode valve, the world's first thermionic device. This inspired invention not only paved the way for today's multimedia electronics industry, but also created the delivery platform for space travel, e-mail and the Internet, not to mention computers.

Thirty-two years after Fleming's invention, in November 1936, the world's first high-definition public service television broadcasts were transmitted by the BBC from Alexandra Palace, positioned on the crest of the Lea Valley's western slopes.

Centring the 2012 Olympic and Paralympic Games in London's Lea Valley will provide a unique opportunity to remind the world that it was the development of electronic communication within the region that has allowed the participating nations to share the message of peace and friendship.

Jim Lewis

CONTENTS

INTRODUCTION

It is probably fair to say that authors who research interesting and little-known historical subjects tend to resist the requests of their readers to produce yet another book highlighting new facts. Then, as in my case, the pressure becomes too great and the research bullet has to be bitten. Once the decision is made there is no turning back and the author is faced with months, sometimes years, of archive research to follow up reader leads and to see if sufficient material exists in a particular subject area to construct an interesting and worthwhile story. While the prospect of the challenge at first may appear daunting, once fully committed and immersed in the work the excitement level builds and it is particularly satisfying when new information comes to light.

In my last three books, I invited readers, particularly teachers and school children, to get involved in Lea Valley projects and also to take on the role of detectives to discover if more interesting stories existed about the region. Some schools and universities rose to the challenge and on a number of occasions I was invited to become involved and also to act as a Lea Valley tour guide. It is occasions like these that make writing doubly rewarding.

Due to considerable local interest, and also the requests by many retailers for reprints of earlier material, the author has been persuaded to deviate from the intentions of the original format used in my earlier Lea Valley books, that of keeping chapters deliberately short, and for this new series I shall include a fuller treatment of many of the subjects. Therefore, it is intended to give each book in the series a particular theme. In this way it is hoped that that the readers' requests will be largely satisfied and also a greater insight into the developments of the region will be achieved.

I have been greatly encouraged to be quoted by prominent writers and broadcasters such as Ian Sinclair and also to receive letters from Dr Adam Hart-Davis saying "I had no idea that the great George Parker Bidder was, no less, 'the maker of modern West Ham'. I told the story in the wilds of Moretonhampstead." The BBC newscaster Mike Embly, once referred to me as the "Lea Valley alarm clock" as

I appear to wake people up to the historic significance of the region. These compliments make the long hours in front of a computer screen and the many years of archive research seem worthwhile and this encourages me to discover and write more about the Lea Valley, its entrepreneurs and its world firsts. Perhaps, sometime in the future the region will no longer be Britain's best-kept secret.

As I am mindful that the forthcoming Olympics will bring many people to the Lea Valley from around the world, who will want to learn a little more about the region, I have decided to include some stories to attract those readers with broader interests beyond that of the subject of industrial heritage.

Jim Lewis

1. THE ROYAL SMALL ARMS FACTORY ENFIELD LOCK – THE EARLY YEARS

In setting the scene, it will also be necessary to highlight the various issues which slowed the rate of progress and innovation within the British small arms manufacturing industry in comparison to the speed of technological achievement attained by its American counterpart particularly in the field of machine tool development. Unfortunately, due to limitations of space, it will not be possible to cover the whole range of influences which affected the British small arms industry in detail. However, it is hoped to show that the path of the British small arms industry towards interchangeability and standardised mass-produced weapons was anything but straightforward.

ESTABLISHING THE ARMOURY

The construction of the small arms factory beside the River Lea at Enfield Lock on the Essex and Middlesex borders came about through a British government initiative. Action to proceed with construction had been provoked by what the Board of Ordnance regarded as the failure of the private gun trade to provide sufficient quantities of weapons for the British Army and Navy during the Napoleonic Wars. By 1816 the factory and houses for the workmen and their families had been completed. Also during this year the barrel branch from the Royal Manufactory at Lewisham was incorporated into the site as water power for the south London armoury began to fail. The lock and finishing sections from Lewisham were integrated later adding to the site's gradual expansion. However, it was not until after some forty years of further building and equipping that the Royal Small Arms Factory (as it was to become known) became capable of producing large quantities of weapons by standardised methods of machine manufacture. Up until the middle of the century the factory acted largely as a research and development establishment, an assembly and small weapon modification shop and a repair facility. Because of the expert knowledge of arms production and assembly contained within the factory, the establishment was also used to monitor the price and quality of finished parts and complete weapons produced by private contractors for the Board of Ordnance.

The large machine room completed circa 1856 with canal, original grinding mill head stream, in the foreground.

Despite the early initiative taken by the British government to control and secure regular supplies of military small arms by building the factory at Enfield Lock, it took over four decades before regular supplies to the armed forces could be guaranteed from this plant. The circumstances responsible for this somewhat ironic situation provide an interesting study, in which it can be shown that it was the private sector and not, as commonly believed, the public sector which was still producing the bulk of military small arms up until circa 1857. Should the reader wish to learn more about the complex series of events which placed the British government in the embarrassing position of being incapable of providing large quantities of small arms by the middle of the century, it is recommended to consult the reference section to this chapter.

THE INFLUENCE OF GEORGE LOVELL

George Lovell was appointed Storekeeper, a position similar to today's General Manager, at Enfield Lock on 1st April 1816, the date coinciding with the barrel branch being moved from Lewisham. Most students of the history of the Royal Small Arms Factory (RSAF) agree that it was Lovell more than any other individual who, with his expertise and dedication, laid the foundations and set the bench marks for quality and reliability which were to become synonymous with the RSAF in later years.

Lovell was determined to improve the tolerance standards of weapons and piece parts delivered to "Ordnance" by the various private contractors. In 1833, armed with a new micrometer he was able to ascertain that the instruments used for measuring the bores of barrels of small arms varied between 0.752 and 0.760 of an inch. He therefore set the standard at 0.754 of an inch, a measurement which would be strictly adhered to in the future. By necessity, increased levels of accuracy call for greater standards of skill and improved manufacturing techniques if high rejection rates are to be avoided. Improvements of this scale in the short term can lead to a decrease in manufacturing output, accounting for a reduction in profit margins. As it might be imagined, Lovell's demands for tolerances to a thousandth of an inch brought considerable criticism from the private contractors. One anonymous observer unhappy with the new imposed standards called Lovell "a cabinet or bedstead maker by trade". Going on, this nameless person criticised the strictness imposed by the "Ordnance" viewers (quality control and inspection personnel) upon the private gun trade which led "to a litigious vexatious nicety of gauging, and finished appearance unknown in the highest finished fowling pieces". He described as absurd "the principle of exact jigging, gauging, moulding and other fantastic accuracies".

Lovell's problems did not subside after his appointment to Inspector of Small Arms in 1840, the most influential position in all aspects of British military weapon design, manufacture, and procurement below that of the Master General of Ordnance. If anything, the personal attacks increased and considerable controversy was to surround his later years. These issues and the consequences of "Ordnance" imposing strict quality standards form part of the complex nature of the British small arms industry, illustrating the somewhat delicate character of the military gun trade, during the first half of the nineteenth century.

"ORDNANCE" DILEMMA

It is clear from the many written accounts of the British gun trade in the period to the middle of the nineteenth century that production was essentially uncoordinated and fragmented, being split mainly between the London and Birmingham private gun makers. As the demand for arms changed during times of military conflict the private-sector gun manufacturing industry suffered not only from the indecisiveness of government policies, but also from the general lack of understanding of their needs and requirements by the "Ordnance" procurement agencies. Skilled men were lost to the industry, sometimes never to return, as many gun makers were unable to find work for their craftsmen or were denied the stability

The church at the Royal Small Arms Factory, Enfield Lock was built circa 1850, closed in 1922 and demolished in 1928.

of long-term "Ordnance" contracts. The apparent reluctance of government to initiate a policy of major intervention into the arms industry was primarily due to the private gun trade's successful lobby of Parliament, which effectively stopped "Ordnance" encroaching into their area of business, but was in part due to the strong influence of the Duke of Wellington, who, as Commander in Chief of the Army, believed that arms themselves needed no improvement, the only improvement required being the degree and extent of the troops' instruction in their use.

In addition, the contract system operated by the Board of Ordnance moved from one of favoured manufacturers to one of open tender at the lowest price. This helped create supply and price difficulties for military weapons, as rejection rates increased and contractors tried to recover lost "Ordnance" business by increasing costs. This helped to deepen the impression that the private sector was incapable of meeting the reasonable demands of "Ordnance". As the middle of the century approached, these were just some of the issues facing both "Ordnance" and the private gun trade.

In October 1853, Mr (later Sir) John Anderson, the chief engineer of the Royal Arsenal at Woolwich, was sent to Enfield and instructed

The tool room at the Royal Small Arms Factory, Enfield Lock during Mafeking celebrations in 1900.

to find out whether the factory was capable of manufacturing bayonets by machinery. Following his visit, Anderson issued a report to which the official response of "Ordnance" was to appoint a committee to consider the whole question of small arms provision for Her Majesty's Service. Lieutenant Colonel Alexander Tulloh, Royal Artillery, Inspector of the Royal Carriage Factory at Woolwich, and Colonel James Archibald Chalmer, R.A., Inspector of Artillery, reported to the committee making the following observations:

> It appears that the system hitherto adopted to procure small arms is so heterogeneous in its character that it could not fail to produce considerable difficulties. The Government establish-ment at Enfield Lock is comparatively small and of a mixed nature, some parts of the work being performed by the establishment, some by contractors; many of the lathes and tools are the property of the workmen; others belonging to the establishment. The men possessing lathes hire them out to other men.
>
> The establishment at Enfield Lock being small, and forming part of the heterogeneous system, is unable to hold that check or control over the contractors to prevent exorbitant demands and serious delays. The principal part of the gun trade upon which

The Telpher Track, circa 1900, used for lifting heavy loads from the barges which brought material to the factory via the site canal, which was connected to the River Lea. Behind the bridge, on the right of the picture, can be seen a loaded coal barge.

> the Government mainly depends for supply in case of emergency, is carried on in Birmingham and London, by men working by hand in wretched cellars and garrets, and great evil arises from the slowness of manufacture.

It can be seen from these findings that the committee was reinforcing the image, already held by "Ordnance", that the small arms industry in Britain was in rather a perilous state. This would appear especially true if one considers the imperial role of Britain in the nineteenth century, and the consequent need to police her far flung empire. Furthermore, for a nation which had been at the heart of the Industrial Revolution it must have been extremely embarrassing for government to witness senior "Ordnance" officers being forced to purchase quantities of arms from continental manufacturers in times of conflict. Having to go abroad to find ways of bridging the gaps brought about by recurring delays and non-fulfilment of military contracts by local industry was clearly an unsatisfactory political outcome.

Further scorn was heaped upon the private gun trade when Sir Thomas Hastings, the Ordnance Principal Storekeeper, in evidence to the committee, read some of the written excuses given by contractors for delays. These were strikes amongst the workmen, difficulty in procuring coal, illness of a skilled artisan, and accident to machinery. It would seem there was little sympathy with the contractors' reasons for delay as Lord Raglan, the Master General of Ordnance, and Sir Thomas Hastings had already formed the view that "Ordnance" should take control of small arms manufacture. They stated:

> they had been guided in their opinion partly by the report of the Commissioners who, during the last year, visited the manufactories of the United States, and partly from communications with Mr Anderson and other persons conversant with machinery.

Reading the report, and considering the evidence from the committee's point of view, it would be difficult to see how they could have reached any other conclusion than for the Board of Ordnance to assume overall responsibility for military small arms manufacture. The past three years had seen a worsening of arms deliveries to "Ordnance" and the commencement of war in the Crimea had heightened pressure for a radical review of procurement. Given that the British armed forces were again placed in the position of being without sufficient quantities of reliable small arms in time of war, as they had been during the Napoleonic conflict, it might be considered strange that by the middle of the century "Ordnance" still relied heavily upon the independent gun trade for its weapon supplies. The private sector, for reasons that will be explained later, had not modernised its methods of manufacture and did not do so until well into the second half of the century, instead relying heavily on traditional manual skills. Only after their hand had been forced through competition from the new government factory at Enfield Lock did the private contractors set up the Birmingham Small Arms company (BSA) in 1861. Further pressure for radical change was heaped on the private sector when "Ordnance" began placing contracts for weapons manufactured only with interchangeable parts.

DELAYING CHANGE

By 1854 the Board of Ordnance had received from the commission led by Lt. Colonel Burn, and the previous year Joseph Whitworth (later Sir), reports detailing the fact that the government armouries in America were employing large amounts of machinery in the manufacture of rifles. The level of mechanisation was reported as being particularly advanced in the operations of forming, shaping, and fitting out gun stocks, formerly considered a highly labour-intensive part of the gun manufacturing process. It was not as if the American government was keeping the technology a secret, for machinery capable of making 130 to 160 gun stocks per day was offered to the Board of Ordnance by an American agent Samuel Cox as early as 1841. In fact the technology for manufacturing large-scale irregular and complex shapes in wood had existed in Britain since the early part of the century. Less than one hundred miles from Enfield, in the Portsmouth dockyards, the relatively complicated ship's pulley block had been manufactured for the

A painting of Marc Isambard Brunel (1769–1849), father of the famous I.K., the designer of the machinery to mass-produce ship's pulley blocks at the Admiralty's Portsmouth Dockyard. To the right of the picture can be seen a model of a mortising machine built by Henry Maudslay.

Navy on a sequence of machines invented by Marc Isambard Brunel (father of Isambard Kingdom Brunel) and built by Henry Maudslay the eminent London engineer. Maudslay's workshops were located within one hour's travel from Enfield, so it is hard to imagine that senior "Ordnance" personnel were ignorant of the available manufacturing technology, especially as it was the Admiralty, another branch of government, which had been responsible for financing the Portsmouth block-making factory. However, the process seems not to have been adopted in Britain for the purpose of manufacturing gun stocks although there is evidence which suggests that the principals were probably "borrowed" by American machine tool inventors and the ideas incorporated into their own designs. These eventually found their way back to Britain via Enfield through the machine tool contract with the Ames Manufacturing Company, Chicopee, Massachusetts, later in the century.

Further examples of differences between British and American manufacturing techniques were observed by "Ordnance" personnel, prominent engineers, and private small arms contractors at the time of the Great Exhibition of 1851 in London's Hyde Park. Here, the American company Robbins and Lawrence had sent six U.S. Army rifles for display and demonstration, all manufactured with parts that interchanged. Samuel Colt exhibited his revolvers which he claimed were made almost entirely by machinery and having parts that were interchangeable for everyone to see. From the evidence it can be seen that both the Board of Ordnance and the private gun makers were aware of the advances made in machine tool technology on the other side of the Atlantic, yet there was still an apparent reluctance to embrace the processes of mechanisation and mass production. For this reluctance to have existed for so long, it would seem fair to conclude that strong and compelling forces were at play.

GRASPING THE NETTLE

When the second commission was sent to America in 1854 led by Lt. Colonel Burn R.A., it had been given quite specific instructions to inspect the different gun factories and to purchase such

The celebrated London engineer, Henry Maudslay (1771–1831) who built Brunel's block-making machines, examples of which can be viewed at the Portsmouth Dockyard and also the Science Museum, London.

machinery and equipment as found necessary for the proposed new factory at Enfield. This was quite a different approach to that of the commission of 1853 which included Joseph Whitworth the distinguished engineer. Whitworth did not go expressly to America to view the gun manufacturers as might be implied by reading some accounts of the visit. Initially he went to attend the New York Industrial Exhibition. This would seem to indicate that in less than a year, the procurement of small arms for the British Army and Navy had reached an extremely critical state. Accompanied by George Wallis, Headmaster of the Birmingham School of Art, Whitworth appears to have taken it upon himself to alter his itinerary, as it is suggested "and while there they extended their enquiries by visiting several establishments, among others the Government Arms Factory at Springfield". This observation is further substantiated in Whitworth's evidence to the 1854 select committee when he stated "that he had not been specially directed to inspect the manufactories of fire-arms, and had not therefore given the close attention to the subject which he would have done if he had foreseen the present inquiry".

The introduction to the 1854 Committee on Machinery's 87-page report sets out their terms of reference and provides an insight into some of the circumstances which helped bring about a marked change of direction by "Ordnance". From the following extract of the report, the reasons can be seen which were to eventually cause "Ordnance" to take on the responsibility of becoming a major manufacturer of military small arms.

> Owing to the delays constantly recurring in the fulfilment of contracts for arms, the high price demanded by contractors, and the inconvenience occasioned to the Service by these causes, the Honourable Board of Ordnance, towards the end of the year 1853, considered it advisable, in order to secure a regular supply of them, to take this branch of manufacture into their own hands, and erect a Government establishment capable of producing muskets in large numbers, and at a moderate price by the introduction of machinery into every part of the manufacturing where it was

Joseph Whitworth (1803–1877) the famous engineer who gave evidence before the Select Committee of 1854 regarding his fact-finding visit to America in 1853.

applicable... Having caused a plan of the building they proposed to erect to be drawn out... [they] set to work as speedily as possible; and hearing from Mr Whitworth and others that machinery was extensively applied to this branch of manufacture in the United States of America, where, on account of the high price of labour, the whole energy of people is directed to improving and inventing labour-saving machinery, the Honourable Board consider it advisable to send over to that country some of their officers, with a view to obtaining every information in their power connected with the manufacture of arms as there conducted, and with the power of buying such machinery as they might consider would be more productive than that used in England for similar purposes.

James Henry Burton (1823–1895), the former Master Armourer at Harpers Ferry, came to Enfield on a five year contract to oversee the installation of the machinery in the large machine room. The bulk of the machinery was purchased from the Ames Manufacturing Company of Chicopee, Massachusetts and Robbins & Lawrence of Windsor, Vermont.

The second commission sent to America placed contracts for machine tools with Robbins & Lawrence of Windsor, Vermont, and the Ames Manufacturing Company, Chicopee, Massachusetts. This latter company produced machinery for fashioning gun stocks, bedding the barrel, and letting in the lock. The machinery proved to be so efficient and reliable that when writing the history of the Royal Small Arms Factory in circa 1930, G.H. Roberts, the then Superintendent proudly wrote:

> It is interesting to note that several of the woodworking machines supplied by the Ames Co. are still in use today and giving good service, in fact one well known Firm of English machinists recently declared that even today they could not improve upon the American machines in the matter of output etc.

Roberts commented further:

> As regards Messrs. Robbins & Lawrence machines, a small Horizontal Milling Machine of their make, probably one of the last of the plant supplied by them has been scrapped within the last year or two although it has not been worked for some time.

From the report of the commission when visiting the U.S. Armoury at Springfield, it would appear that their decision to purchase what must be considered a substantial quantity of machinery, was influenced by at least two important factors: the sequenced operation of the gun stock forming machinery; and the ability of a workman to randomly assemble arms from parts taken from weapons manufactured over a ten year period. To oversee the installation and the commissioning of the machinery at Enfield Lock, James H. Burton, former Master Armourer of Harpers Ferry Armoury, was brought to England on a five-year contract.

The bell, which was cast at the Royal Brass Foundry at Woolwich, originally hung in the tower of the large machine room after the building was completed in 1856.

ENFIELD COMES OF AGE

The years 1855 to 1859 saw the rapid expansion of building at Enfield Lock. Construction work was carried out by the Royal Engineers under the supervision of Captain Thomas Bernard Collison, R.E. During this period the large machine room was completed specifically to house the new machinery, much of which was purchased in America by the 1854 commission. The plant was designed for an estimated annual production of 130,000 muskets and bayonets. In the early years, although expenditure on land, buildings, machinery, and gas works amounted to £315,000, the success of the plant was such that, according to Roberts, by 1862 this sum together with depreciation of £48,000 was said to have been entirely repaid by the reduced cost of production.

Before 1861 the energy source for the Enfield manufactory had been water taken from the River Lea to drive two 18-foot-diameter cast-iron water wheels, each having an estimated output of 46 horsepower. The design of the drive, which did not incorporate governors, was reported to have made the outputs very irregular. Primarily, the main function of the water wheels was to run the barrel grinding shop which, according to reports, continued with this source of power until 1887. Amazingly it has been recorded that the use of the traditional grit grindstone was not finally discontinued until circa 1926.

Red sandstone grinding wheel, formerly from the grinding shop, Royal Small Arms Factory, Enfield Lock.

In 1852 a new Barrel Rolling Plant was installed and by 1853 Roberts reported that the factory capacity was 50,000 muskets and 3,000 swords per annum. Prior to this, and using only an average of 25 horsepower before steam was introduced, it was claimed that the production rate of the Enfield factory had been in the order of 7,000 small arms and 1,500 swords annually. However, the historian of industrial technology Professor Tim Putnam, when referring to George Lovell, suggests that "the number of complete weapons in his period never approached that figure". This, he concludes, is based upon the assumption that Enfield was using a number of individual components purchased from the private contractors rather than manufacturing the complete arm in-house.

The barrel room at the Royal Small Arms Factory, Enfield Lock during Mafeking celebrations in 1900.

Once the American machine tools had been installed at Enfield, not only was there a dramatic increase in arms production, but their introduction also made the RSAF the first British plant to be able to claim that their machined parts were so accurate that they could be interchanged between weapons. This is the first true example of a British factory using mass production techniques, as defined by the manufacture of standardised machine-made parts that interchanged completely, rather than those which are made to fit on an individual basis, usually by hand finishing. The new system of manufacture was so successful that by year ending 30th June 1860 the output of rifles alone had increased to 90,707, an average of 1,744 per week, later to go up to 1,900. By the year 1861, 1,700 men were employed at the plant and it is recorded that the large machine room (currently the Grade II listed building with the clock tower and interpretation centre) was driven by two 40 horsepower steam engines with Fairbairn expansion gear, while in the barrel mill a 70 horsepower steam engine was employed along with the existing water wheels.

The remains of old grinding machines, excavated in 1968, showing castings placed in them before the floor was boarded over circa 1914–1918.

The view, facing north, showing remains of old grinding machines after excavation in building No. 86, later designated building No. 64.

It would therefore seem that one could proclaim with confidence that the "American system of manufactures" (as it has popularly become known) had truly arrived at Enfield and was seen to be working.The private gun trade had yet to respond to the challenge of producing military weapons with standardised and interchangeable parts by the extensive use of machine tools.

The large machine room in 1998, Grade II listed, with the canal, opened up as a water feature, and the barge *Royal Ordnance* in the foreground.

In this chapter a number of issues have been highlighted which have arisen out of the installation of the "American system" at Enfield Lock. Should the reader wish to gain a deeper knowledge of the complexities surrounding the British small arms industry in the nineteenth century, an analysis, together with the effects, problems, and advantages for both the Board of Ordnance and the independent gun trade, can be derived from the recommended reading.

The Royal Small Arms Factory at Enfield Lock lasted for over one hundred and seventy years, providing arms for the Allied forces in two world wars. Many of the famous Lee-Enfield magazine rifles can still be seen in use around the world today.This is a lasting tribute to the quality of the product produced by the RSAF workforce. It was a sad day for manufacturing in the Lea Valley when the factory's closure was announced in August 1987. During its life the factory created work for generations of local people - in many cases whole families. It has often been said that once you had served an apprenticeship or had been employed at the RSAF, your skills would be in great demand from other employers.

The Royal Small Arms Factory night shift, technical staff, Enfield Lock, 7th December 1918.

The Royal Small Arms Factory officers and technical staff, Enfield Lock, 7th December 1918.

Armourers second football team circa 1910. On the extreme right in uniform is "Jack" or "Spud" Murphy (1894–1965).

REFERENCES

Bailey, De Witt, "George Lovell and The Growth of the RSAF Enfield", paper presented at MA Day School, Middlesex University, 4th July 1992.

Blackmore, Howard L., "Military Gun Manufacturing in London and the Adoption of Interchangeability", *Arms Collecting* Vol. 29, No. 4, November 1991.

Cottesloe, Colonel, Lord, C.B., "Notes on the History of the Royal Small Arms Factory, Enfield Lock", *Army Historical Research* Volume 12, undated, probably circa 1932.

Gilbert, K.R., "The Ames Recessing Machine: A Survivor of the Original Enfield Rifle Machinery", *Technology and Culture*, Vol. 4, Part 2, 1963.

House of Lords Record Office, London, "Report of the Committee on the Machinery of the United States of America, Presented to the House of Commons, in Pursuance of their Address of 10th July, 1855".

Institute of Civil Engineers, Minutes of Proceedings, Vol. 27, London 1867-1868, "Address of the President", C.H. Gregory.

Putnam, Tim & Weinbren, Dan, "A Short History of the Royal Small Arms Factory Enfield", Middlesex University, 1992.

Royal Ordnance, Nottingham (archive now located at the library of the Royal Armouries, Leeds) "Notes on the History of the Royal Small Arms Factory, Enfield Lock", Unsigned typed manuscript circa 1930, accompanied by a memorandum, dated 24th December 1930, signed G.H. Roberts [Superintendent RSAF 1922-31], clearly showing that he is the author of the RSAF history.

Select Committee on Small Arms, "Report from the Select Committee on Small Arms", House of Commons, May 1854, (184. 251).

Whitworth, J. & Wallis, G., *The Industry of the United States in Machinery, Manufacturers and Useful and Ornamental Arts*, 1854.

Note 1

There does appear to be some confusion with regard to the actual date when the RSAF was first established. R.H. Roberts in his notes suggests the establishment was, "about the year 1804". Colonel Lord Cottesloe, C.B. confirms this date in his article, "Notes on the History of the Royal Small Arms Factory, Enfield Lock", Volume 12 of *Army Historical Research*. This is not particularly surprising as Cottesloe bases most of his article on the notes of Roberts. A. Robinson and J. Burnby's Occasional Paper No. 50 for the Edmonton Hundred Historical Society, "Guns and Gun Powder in Enfield", suggests that negotiations were started for the land to build the new manufactory on 14th July 1811. George Lovell (appointed as Storekeeper at Enfield Lock, 1st April 1816), in his report on the background and present state of the Enfield factory (W.O.44/682) to Sir Henry Hardinge (Board of Ordnance), lists the following under "Lands": "4 Acres, 2 Rods, 5 Poles of Sedgy and Swampy Ground adjoining the River, purchased therewith from William Sotherby, Esq. in 1808."

Note 2

There has been some confusion as to who actually led the 1854 Commission on Machinery during their American tour. For example, David A. Hounshell, in his book *From the American System to Mass Production 1800-1932: The Development of Manufacturing Technology in the United States* (Baltimore:

the Johns Hopkins University Press, 1984, p.4), suggests that John Anderson was the leader.

However, it is clear from the "Report of the Committee on the Machinery of the United States of America, Presented to the House of Commons, in Pursuance of their Address of the 10th July, 1855", p.2 (548), (House of Lords Record Office, London) that Anderson was not the leader. Here it is clearly documented that Lieutenant Colonel Burn, Royal Artillery, who held the position of Assistant Inspector of Artillery at Woolwich, had been appointed to lead the commission. A communication dated 13th February 1854, from the Office of Ordnance shows that the Secretary to the Board of Ordnance, J. Wood, had passed on the Board's instruction to Burn stating "I am to add that Lieutenant Warlow, Royal Artillery, and Mr. Anderson, have been instructed to proceed thither on the 4th March next, and to place themselves under your direction; and I am to request you will give them such instructions previous to your departure as you may consider necessary".

Interestingly, in the unpublished history of the RSAF written by G.H. Roberts he mistakenly lists a Major Turborville accompanying Lt. Colonel Burn, Lieutenant Warlow and Mr Anderson as part of the commission sent to America in 1854. All the documentary evidence, which includes the "Report of the Committee on the Machinery of the United States of America", lists only the latter three members. In fact, this report, which describes their findings during the tour of American manufacturing establishments in 1854 and was presented to the House of Commons "in Pursuance of their Address of the 10th July, 1855", is signed only by Burn, Warlow and Anderson.

Roberts' mistake is curious as he clearly had access to material which may not have been freely available to other historians at the time. In the preface to his "Notes on the History of the Royal Small Arms Factory, Enfield Lock", he states "The writer wishes to place on record his indebtedness to Sir Herbert J. Creedy, Secretary of the War Office, for permission to consult a number of War Office records".

Apart from this one transgression, Roberts is to be congratulated for having the interest and enthusiasm to begin assembling the facts which have assisted later historians with their researches into the history of the RSAF.

Note 3

The probable explanation for Lovell being called a "bedstead maker" is that in the late 1820s, to keep the Enfield factory going, Lovell took on all kinds of work, including making bedsteads.

It is worth noting that George Lovell, the first Storekeeper at the RSAF, should not to be confused with Frederick Lovell, his brother, Clerk 1824, or Francis George Lovell, his son, Assistant Inspector of Arms 1843. Robert Lovell, another son, also worked in the industry.

Note 4

For further reading and an in-depth study of the reasons which delayed the introduction of weapons made with interchangeable parts see PhD Thesis by James H. Lewis "The Development of the Royal Small Arms Factory (Enfield Lock) and its Influence Upon Mass Production Technology and Product Design c.1820–c.1880". Copies of the thesis can be viewed by appointment by contacting Middlesex University Library Services or the Royal Armouries Library, Leeds.

2. THE NATIONAL GUN-STOCK CRISIS – GEORGE LOVELL TO THE RESCUE

One of the major obstacles to the continuous production of small arms in nineteenth-century Britain was the erratic supply of fully seasoned walnut gun-stock blanks. The main reason for these shortages was the length of the wood seasoning process which could take up to three years to complete (some estimates have suggested as much as five) by natural drying methods. Clearly an urgent solution had to be found if Britain wanted to equip her army and navy with serviceable weapons. It was George Lovell (1789–1854), the Board of Ordnance Inspector of Small Arms and formerly the Storekeeper at the Royal Small Arms Factory (RSAF) at Enfield Lock, who came to the rescue.

In February 1848, Lovell wrote a report after visiting the firm of Davis & Symington's in London, where he examined the process of "desiccation of wood and other substances by the application of currents of heated air". Lovell reported that the process consisted of having a ventilated room 24 feet by 18 feet and 15 feet to the roof, formed with double walls and doors to "prevent warmth escaping laterally". He also reported that the floor was constructed of York paving on a bed of concrete and that in one corner of the room stood a stove furnace which had a 26-foot chimney.

The system described by Lovell had consisted of a fan located in an external wall that was driven by a strap from a drum in an adjoining building. Outside air was drawn in by the fan and fed through an iron pipe which then passed in a series of loops within the furnace. This action heated the air which was then fed to warm-air ducts in the floor, where it escaped through perforated iron plates. Wood to be dried was placed on racks within the chamber and the warm air, through convection, rose around it, carrying the expelled moisture upward and out of the building via ventilators in the roof.

Lovell was a methodical and thorough man and he therefore decided to test the system fully himself. First, he took thirty gun stocks that were partly seasoned (fifteen months in store) and thirty that were "quite fresh cut and full of sap". These were carefully

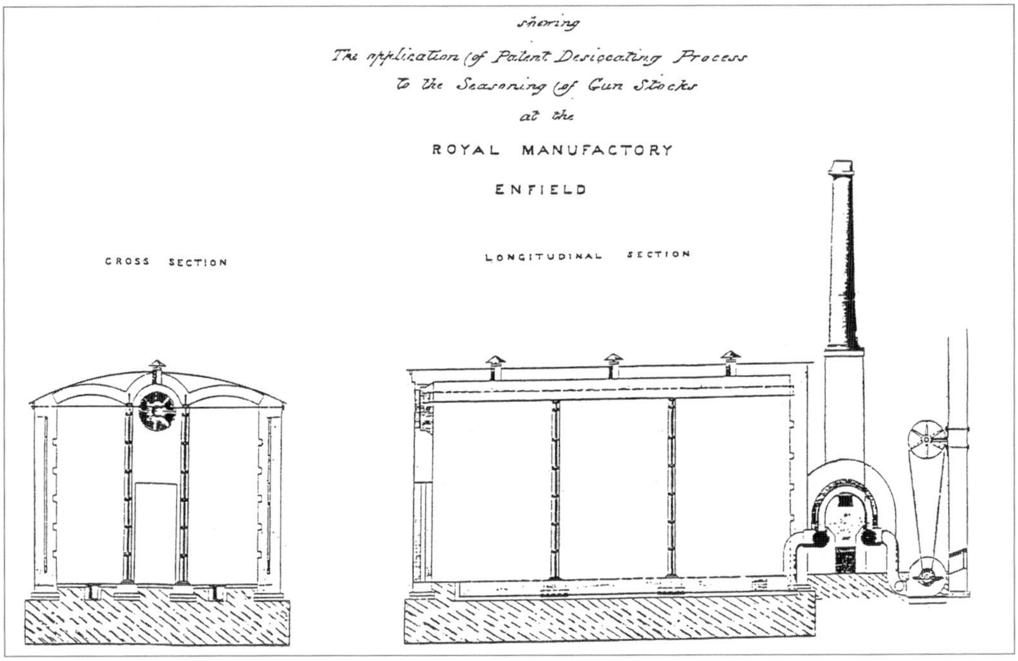

A plan of the Davis & Symington's patent process gun-stock seasoning chamber, circa 1848, that was installed at the Royal Small Arms Factory at Enfield Lock.

weighed and put in the drying room for ten days at a temperature of 110 to 114 degrees Fahrenheit. The following results were obtained and recorded:

Stocks	Weight before process	After process	Weight loss
30 Half seasoned	240lbs. 14.5ozs.	206lbs. 13ozs.	34lbs. 1.5ozs.
30 Fresh	295lbs. 10.5ozs.	207lbs. 1.5ozs.	88lbs. 9ozs.

Second, the sixty stocks were exposed to the air in the stock store and in the first seven days they had increased in weight by 2.5% as they absorbed moisture from the atmosphere. Lovell commented, "as might be expected from the hygroscopic state of the wood". But over the next eighteen days the stocks had only increased by 1.5%. Further experiments by Lovell found that by exposing six stocks dried naturally and six dried by "the process", both for thirty days, the former increased in weight by 3.6% and the latter only 1.55%. Not allowing the experiment to rest there, Lovell took it to the next stage by dispatching the stocks to the trade without informing them that they had been hot air processed. In his report he gives his reasons as follows:

> With a view to collect the opinion of working men upon the state of the wood; I directed 15 of the desiccated stocks to be set up into musquets in London, 15 at Birmingham and 15 at the Royal Manufactory at Enfield. My own view of the subject is that

> by quickly inspissating the albumence and juices of the wood at the same time that humidity or mere water is driven off, the wood is rendered tougher than when dried more slowly in the natural way. …but the experiments may have satisfied me that the process offers by far the best means of seasoning wood quickly that has yet come under my observation; and I think that it may be adopted with every prospect of advantage to the Services: more especially at the present moment when the demand for dry musquet stocks is so pressing.

On the strength of Lovell's findings a drying chamber was built at Enfield, the work being completed in September 1848. However, all had not been plain sailing for the project, for it had taken several months of dealing with frustrating bureaucracy and the exchange of countless letters between Lovell, the Board of Ordnance, and Davis & Symington's (known as the Patent Desiccating Company) over costs and royalty payments associated with the process. Specifications for the drying chamber were altered with the Inspector General of Fortifications becoming involved. He then went on to recommend that the "chamber should be isolated and not built against [the] end of [the] water wheel house". Also he stated that the fan was to be increased in size so as to double as substitute bellows for the smith's forges, powered by a belt from the water wheel, saving the cost of a steam engine. However, from the changes, other structural costs emerged and the original estimate was increased from £630 to £710 to take account of the end-wall brickwork specification being revised upward to 18 inches. The estimated time to complete the work also increased from six to eight weeks.

Plan showing how the fan in the seasoning chamber would be driven by a belt and pulley attached to drive shafting. The power came from the mill wheel in the barrel grinding shop.

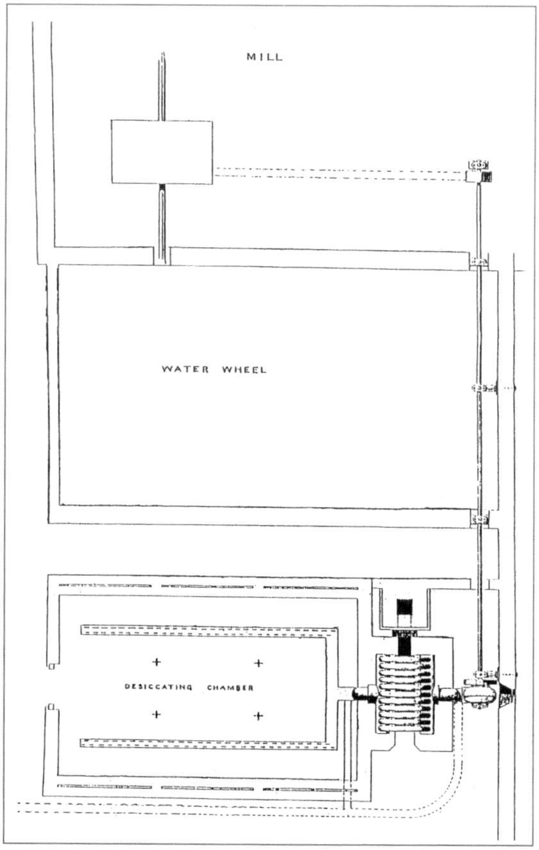

Towards the end of the correspondence, Lovell emerges as the clever politician who is determined to get his way by bringing the matter to a head. After putting forward a range of options, the Patent Desiccating Company offered a compromise solution by dropping their demand for a substantial payment to use their process. The Company now proposed a package that would include a corrugated roof for the chamber rather than an asphalted one.

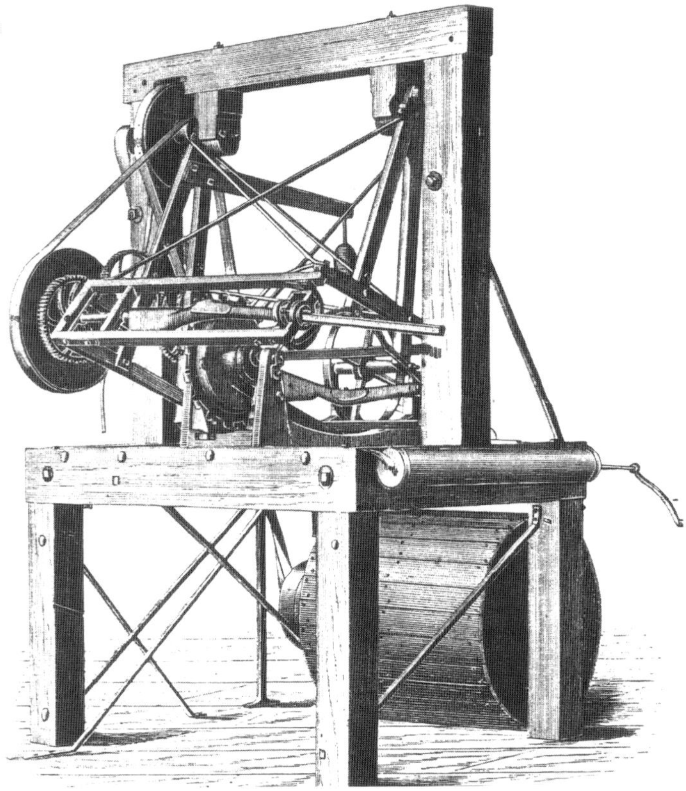

An engraving of Thomas Blanchard's gun-stocking machine, circa 1818. Note the wooden frame. This machine can be seen in the Springfield Armoury Museum, Springfield, Massachusetts.

Lovell wrote to the Board of Ordnance on 3rd April stating "I do not think that the sum now asked by the Company is unreasonable; and I would therefore take the liberty to advise that their offer be accepted". A few days later Lovell was again writing to the Board of Ordnance and playing his political trump card:

> I am under the necessity of suspending the issue of materials for setting up Extra Service Musquets at the Tower, in consequence of the store of seasoned gun stocks being entirely exhausted and that there are no more left at Birmingham than will meet the issues for about three weeks.

Twisting the screw a little tighter, Lovell recommended to the Board of Ordnance that 15,000 stocks be sent to the Patent Desiccating Company for drying at £12 10s per thousand, total cost £187 10s. This quantity Lovell believed would be sufficient to bridge the gap until the erection of the chamber at Enfield. Pushing home his advantage Lovell makes the point:

> I would beg the Hon Board's earliest decision upon this latter point; because it would be otherwise absolutely necessary to

An Ames Manufacturing Company of Chicopee, Massachusetts, gun-stocking machine, circa 1853, purchased by the Board of Ordnance for the Royal Small Arms Factory at Enfield Lock. These machines were based on Thomas Blanchard's original design and improved by the American engineer Cyrus Buckland.

continue the seasoning by the Company to at least a number of 60,000 more in the present financial year at an expense of not less than £750. The Board will perceive from this that the adoption of the proposition of the 3rd instant will prove less expensive even within the present year.

From the correspondence it would seem fair to conclude that it was not the supply of gun stocks per se that presented the bottleneck to arms production, but the supply of seasoned stocks. It would have been difficult, if not impossible, for Ordnance always to calculate their annual requirement of fully seasoned wood accurately to meet every unforeseen contingency. This would have been made more acute as natural curing, as suggested, could take upwards of three years to complete. Therefore the installation of the desiccating chamber at Enfield would have provided one of the most significant breakthroughs in the ability to mass-produce small arms by dramatically reducing timescales in material acquisition. Of course having a reasonable quantity of seasoned stocks in store would also allow "Ordnance" to be more flexible in the planning process, making the annual calculations for arms less traumatic as this particular bottleneck would have effectively been removed.

An Ames Manufacturing Company lock-bedding machine of the type used at the Royal Small Arms Factory in the mid-nineteenth century.

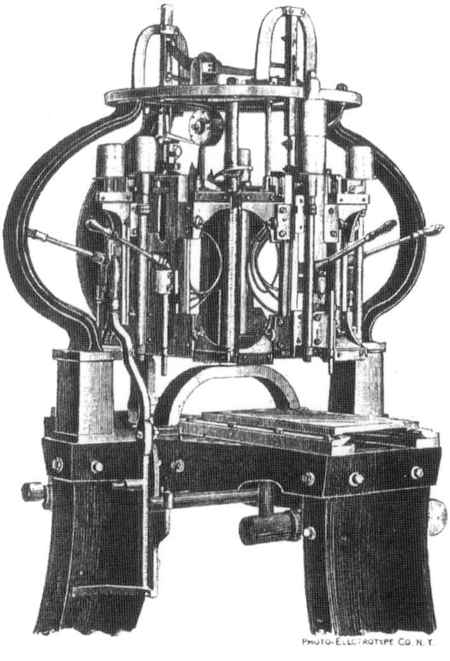

All the research carried out to date would seem to suggest that the Royal Small Arms Factory at

The Royal Small Arms Factory screw department during the Mafeking celebrations of 1900.

Enfield Lock was unique in being the only national arms manufactory in the world to have a gun-stock drying facility constructed onsite. George Lovell deserves recognition for this remarkable achievement and for the considerable contribution he made to the British gun trade by forcing them to adopt methods of standardisation in the manufacture of small arms.This prepared the way for the mass production of weapons with interchangeable parts manufactured by machine.

The Royal Small Arms Factory stocking shop during the Mafeking celebrations of 1900.

REFERENCES

Battison, Edwin A., interview, 22nd August 1994.

National Archive, Kew, "Gun Stock Making Machine de Barros Ignacio", 1849, letter from de Barros to R. Bayham, 7th August 1849, reference WO 44/623/199.

House of Lords Record Office, London, "Report of the Committee on the Machinery of the United States of America, Presented to the House of Commons, in Pursuance of their Address of the 10th July, 1855", pp.39–42.

Note

Edwin Battison is an acknowledged American expert on machine tools and the nineteenth-century gun trade in the United States. During the interview with regard to the issues surrounding the curing of gun stocks, Battison ventured the opinion that there was a possibility that the Springfield armoury in Massachusetts had used kiln-dried wood in the first half of the nineteenth century. However, subsequent research by the author suggests that this was not the case. According to the United States of America Ordnance Department, Washington, *Regulations for The Inspection of Small Arms*, 1823, page 14, "No stocks should be used, which have not been cut from the plank at least three years, and have been stored in a dry place for two years. Kiln dried, or steamed stocks, should not be received." Further support for this directive can be observed later in the century in the article "The Armoury at Springfield", by Jacob Abbott, *Harper's New Monthly Magazine*, No. XXVI, July 1852, Vol. V. Under the section entitled "The Stocking Shop", the author states, "The wood used for gun stocks in this country is the black walnut, and as this wood requires to be seasoned some years before it is used, an immense store of it is kept on hand at the Armoury – sufficient in fact for four years consumption".

Therefore, it would appear that, at least between the years 1823 and 1852, kiln-dried wood was not used in the manufacture of gunstocks at Springfield.

3. "ORDNANCE" FAILINGS, SUPPLYING SMALL ARMS FOR THE CRIMEAN WAR, THE START OF THE TRADE UNION AND THE GROWING PROMINENCE OF THE ENFIELD FACTORY

The mid-1850s represent one of the most critical periods in the history of British small arms manufacture, one in which apparently unconnected events have together shown remarkable catalytic effects. By focussing attention on this period we are able to identify not only the early changes to manufacturing technology and work-place organisation but also the difficulties experienced by a nationalised industry overseen by incompetent or inexperienced government bureaucrats. Perhaps surprisingly, parallels can be drawn between some of these nineteenth-century events and those which have occurred in the small arms industry of today, at the beginning of the twenty-first century. A recent example which occurred in the mid-1980s helps to illustrate the point. On this occasion, government bureaucracy interfered with the department responsible for the production of the Enfield SA80 (Light Support Weapon) and caused confusion amongst the manufacturing staff. The action created a six-week production delay, as government officials, who had not properly investigated an isolated complaint of premature weapon discharge, prompted design changes to the gun.

A CONFUSED PICTURE

Prior to the expansion of the "Ordnance" factory at Enfield in the mid-1850s, the establishment being the first British manufactory to adopt the technology and principles of mass production by the system of interchangeable parts, the vision of the English gun trade portrayed by research is one of an industry lacking direction and severely stricken by turmoil and confusion. As the middle of the century was reached, the mounting pressure from sections within "Ordnance" for control of the military small arms industry finally took hold, motivated in the main by the requirements of war.

Following the Great Exhibition of 1851, the continuing debate between the private gun trade and the Board of Ordnance over weapon deliveries and quality standards was becoming more acrimonious, the arguments spilling over into the evidence given before the Select Committee on Small Arms in 1854. As we have already discussed, many engineers and entrepreneurs had visited the exhibition held within the Crystal Palace and marvelled at such American exhibits as the Sharpe's rifle manufactured by Robbins & Lawrence and the revolvers of Colonel Colt made with standardised parts. However, there were some established gun makers, like Mr W. Scott of Birmingham, who would not entertain the idea that large quantities of machine-made products could be accurately produced without the involvement of skilled artisans. When asked by the select committee if he thought it possible to produce parts by machines which could "fit into one another perfectly without a great deal of manual labour", he replied "Certainly not; by no means; it is impossible".

The scene inside the Great Exhibition with the upper galleries to the left and right and also showing the vast expanse of glass in the roof. It was the extensive use of glass in the construction of the building that provoked the journalists of *Punch* magazine to coin the name "Crystal Palace".

Joseph Whitworth's fact-finding tour of America in 1853, when he and George Wallis visited a number of diverse manufacturing establishments, and the subsequent visit by the commission led by Colonel Burn in 1854, which placed substantial contracts for arms-production machinery with American manufacturers, were all intertwined with "Ordnance" seeking ways to overcome the problems they were encountering with arms procurement. At the time, the British private gun trade were allegedly falling behind with military deliveries and failing the quality standards set by

A lithograph of the Main Avenue within the "Crystal Palace" showing some of the many exhibits that had been supplied by British and foreign manufacturers.

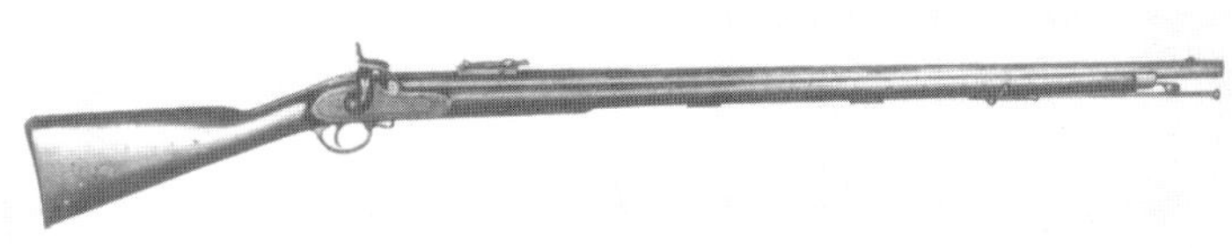

Rifle Musket Minié Pattern 1851 (0.702 inch). This was the standard military weapon before the introduction of the Enfield Pattern 1853.

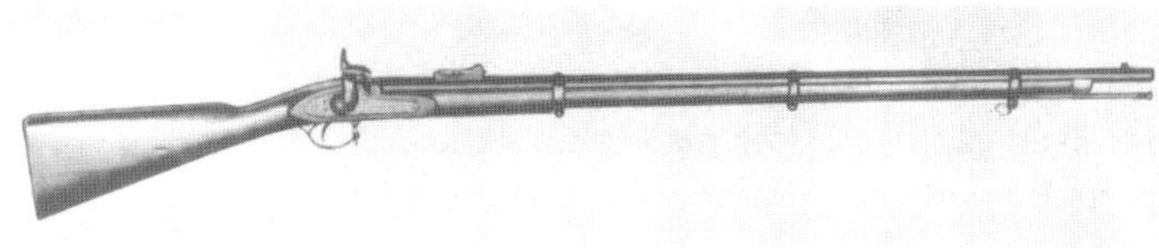

The Enfield Rifle Pattern 1853 (0.577 inch). This was the first weapon to be manufactured with interchangeable parts at Enfield Lock.

"Ordnance". The situation was further complicated by the introduction of the new Pattern 1853 Enfield rifle to replace the existing service 1851 Minié and there was evidence of "Ordnance" withholding the new pattern from which the contractors had to copy. Out of this chaotic state there was mounting pressure upon "Ordnance" to equip soldiers in the Crimea with decent serviceable weapons, not only rifles but also swords and bayonets.

With the build up of hostilities between Russia and Turkey in 1853 and war between them eventually breaking out in October of that year, it was obvious that a major response would be required from small arms manufacturers. This came when Britain and France entered the conflict in March 1854 after declaring war upon Russia.

UNPREPARED FOR BATTLE

During what must be viewed as a critical period in the life of the British small arms industry, correspondence between military regiments and "Ordnance" for the years 1854 to 1855 exposes serious flaws in the "Ordnance" supply chain. These letters indicate quite graphically how fragile the position of Britain really was in arming her troops in time of war. It also illustrates that almost forty years after the establishment of the government armoury at Enfield Lock in response to the parlous state of the indigenous military small arms industry at the time of the Napoleonic Wars, Britain was still unprepared for conflict.

A set of measuring gauges for the Enfield Rifle Pattern 1853. These precision gauges, which took skilled toolmakers months to make, were to ensure that tight manufacturing tolerances were strictly maintained. Also included are gauges for the measurement of lance and pike.

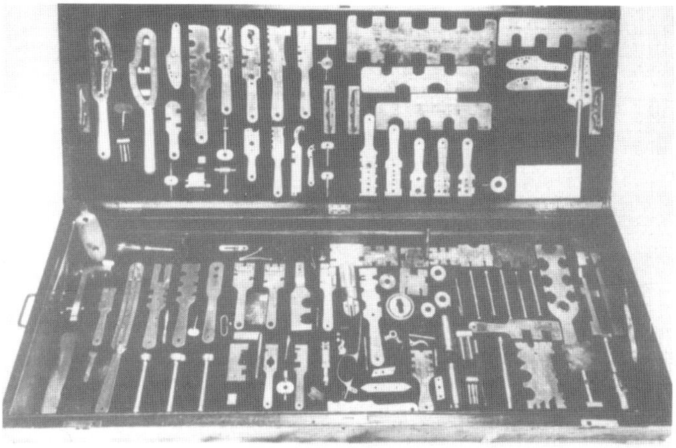

The position is clearly illustrated in a letter dated 14th July 1854 from Lieutenant Colonel Griffith commanding Second Dragoons in Manchester to Joseph Wood the Secretary to the Board of Ordnance, complaining, it would seem not unreasonably, about the poor state of his regiment's weapons. Griffith wrote, "The whole of the Carbines require to be replaced, most of them being worn out from long use. The Victoria Carbines have been mostly in use for 14 years being issued in 1840". Further complaints were made about the "unserviceable" state of the regiment's swords.

In March 1854 similar criticisms had been raised by the 11th Hussars serving in Ireland. Soon Griffith and his men were to embark for the Crimea without replacement Carbines or swords, 180 new pattern swords finally being issued to the Second Dragoons at their Manchester barrack on 1st August after they had already sailed to the front. When the mistake was eventually realised, the swords were dispatched to the Crimea by the Cleopatra on 11th November. Sadly the error was a costly one, as a communication from the War Department dated 13th December to Joseph Wood shows, quoting Colonel Griffith as follows:

> Swords are very defective – as in our engagement, when our men made a thrust with the sword, they all but, and would not go into a man's body, and many of our poor fellows got badly wounded and some lost their lives entirely from the miserable state of their arms. They were quite good enough for home service, but quite unfit for active service.

Unfortunately this was not the end of the Second Dragoon's problems. Colonel Griffith was to write again on the 25th April 1855, reminding Joseph Wood that, before embarkation to the Crimea, the Adjutant General's letters of 18th and 22nd July 1854 had placed requisitions for carbines and swords. The Board of Ordnance correspondence dated 25th July clearly shows that they had no means of supplying this trivial amount of 286 carbines which Griffith had requested. A note scribbled on the back of Griffith's communication dated 26th April 1855 by an S. Roper, states "There is no longer any difficulty in supplying the 286 Victoria Carbines requested by 2nd Dragoons". This was nine months after the original order was placed.

From this episode it is probably fair to conclude that it was Enfield that had responsibility for manufacturing this modest amount of arms, as it was probable that such a small contract would not have been worth putting out to tender. Had this been done, then the delay in supplying the weapons would no doubt have been longer. The competitive nature of the contract system would have required "Ordnance" to distribute and vet the various incoming bids from the private sector and this would have taken time to study and process. Interestingly, this episode also provides a clue to the time required for a factory to adapt to the manufacture of a weapon which was not part of the current production programme. Given the urgency of war, and remembering the weapon was not new and had previously been in production, the incident serves as a general indication of the length of time and the difficulties involved in organising men, mechanisms and material.The introduction of a totally new pattern would no doubt take considerably longer to organise and reach full-scale production capacity. New jigs and gauges would have to be made and, of course, machine operators and other personnel would take time to become fully proficient and familiar with the work.

Bayonet and sword testing at Enfield in the 1850s. Rigorous testing of bayonets and swords was introduced for all "Ordnance" contracts after reports of weapons failure at the Crimean.

The complaint relating to poor-quality swords was investigated by R.W. Gunner, the Inspector of Small Arms at the Birmingham

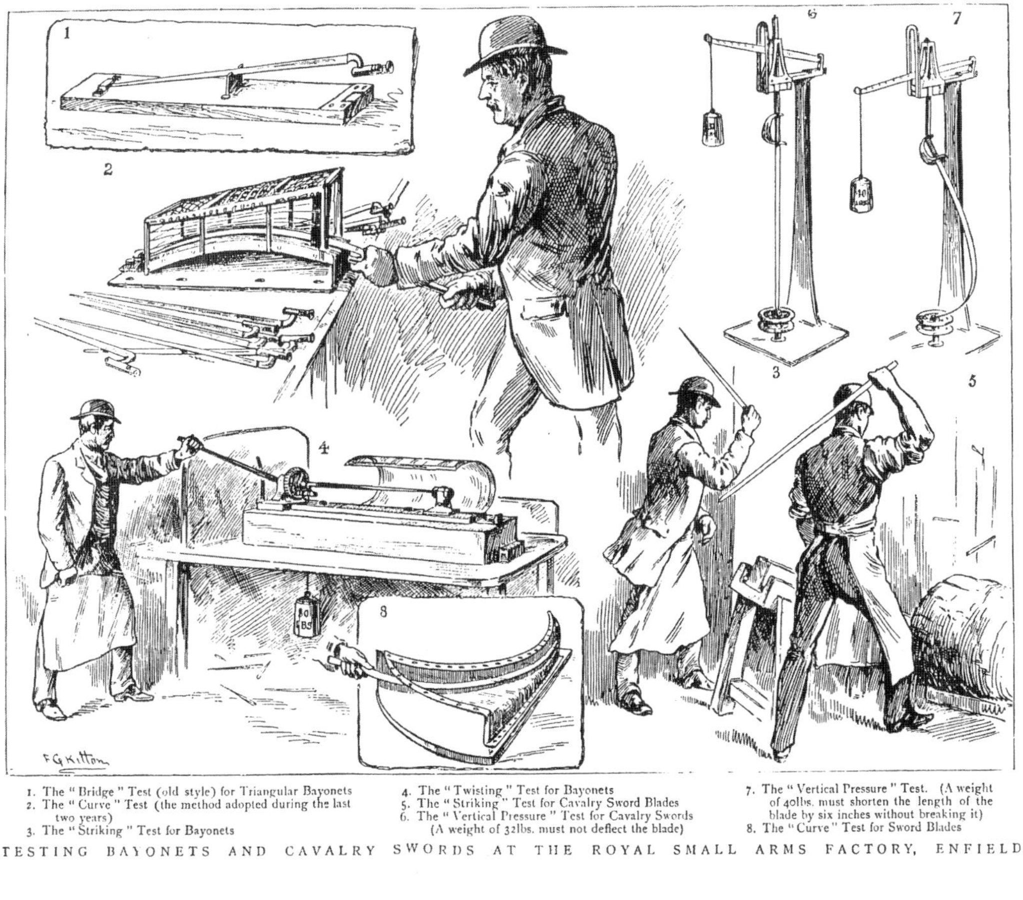

1. The "Bridge" Test (old style) for Triangular Bayonets
2. The "Curve" Test (the method adopted during the last two years)
3. The "Striking" Test for Bayonets
4. The "Twisting" Test for Bayonets
5. The "Striking" Test for Cavalry Sword Blades
6. The "Vertical Pressure" Test for Cavalry Swords (A weight of 32lbs. must not deflect the blade)
7. The "Vertical Pressure" Test. (A weight of 40lbs. must shorten the length of the blade by six inches without breaking it)
8. The "Curve" Test for Sword Blades

TESTING BAYONETS AND CAVALRY SWORDS AT THE ROYAL SMALL ARMS FACTORY, ENFIELD

"Ordnance" office. He reported, "Soon after the introduction of this Pattern in the year 1822 it was found after a careful course of experimental trials that any of the tests beyond those above described was attended with excessive and unnecessary loss either from breakage or failure in elasticity in the fabrication of the blades". Gunner went on to say that the "New Pattern" swords are subject to more stringent tests, the implication being that it was known the military were equipped with inferior weapons and nothing had been done in the forty years of relative peace to rectify the situation. The incident and other reports of poor quality provoked the Master General of Ordnance, Viscount Hardinge, to set up a committee of cavalry officers to look at the current stocks of swords in store and those in the process of manufacture both at Enfield and Birmingham. In addition to the standard tests, Gunner requested the committee to test the weapons more severely. This they did by "proving the cutting on a bar of iron and the point against a brick wall, without injury in any case to the Swords". After taking evidence from the Inspector of Small Arms and the "Superintendents of the Royal Manufactory", the committee reported, in January 1855, that, in their opinion, "the whole of these weapons are made of the best possible materials and they consider them excellent Swords and fit for any service". This statement was made after four of the Enfield swords and one from Birmingham (over two percent of those examined), failed the test. The committee concluded that in "each instance the fracture was not caused by flaw or softness of metal, but rather from being too highly tempered". While technically the analysis may have been correct, it would be hard to imagine that soldiers in the heat of combat would be interested in the precise nature of the fault. Weapon failure for any reason would have been unacceptable; what soldiers required was reliable weapons in which they could have confidence. Perhaps, at the time, "Ordnance" officers had not appreciated the fact that battles are often won on the factory floor through the quality and quantity of weapons supplied to the troops. The "Ordnance" committee,

A painting of an officer of the 10th Hussars at the Crimean with a curved sword that was possibly manufactured at Enfield.

detached from the horrors of war, declared on completion of their investigation that the present swords were "fit for any service".

From researching the considerable correspondence on the Crimea, it is clear that soldiers had been sent to the front ill equipped for combat with old-issue arms, tragically discovering the inadequacy of their weapons in battle. The failure of the swords in action might indicate that one hundred percent testing and inspection was not being carried out - or perhaps some had escaped the view, either deliberately or by accident.

SUPPLY AND WEAPON PROBLEMS

From our discussion it can be seen that there was a whole catalogue of poor organisation, mismanagement and incompetence surrounding the procurement and supply of small arms to soldiers on active service. Furthermore, it would appear that there was a complete lack of understanding by members of the Board of Ordnance relating to the necessary timescales required by the small arms industry to prepare and schedule the production of new weapons. Apart from senior "Ordnance" personnel in the business of arms procurement having little understanding of how a manufacturing facility operated, it was also apparent that there was a failure to grasp the simple logistics of supplying the troops at the front. The Army in the Crimea had wanted weapons of standard calibre to ease problems in the ammunition supply chain. This would have eliminated the confusion brought about through the issue of more than one size of ammunition. It can readily be deduced from the correspondence between "Ordnance" and the different regiments that at least three types of weapon were in service with the frontline troops, all having different calibre bores. Such a mix of weapons of incompatible calibre had introduced severe supply difficulties for the Army. The authorities had tried to resolve these problems on a makeshift basis by keeping batches of the 1851 Minié and Enfield Pattern 1853 muskets separate. These were then issued to different regiments. By knowing where the various weapon types were, it was hoped that this would avoid mistakes of wrong ammunition being delivered to the regiments.

With the issue of the new smaller-calibre (0.577in.) Pattern 1853 it would appear that some of the former strategic advantages of warfare had been lost. For example, Major E.G.B. Reynolds has argued that "It was considered an advantage to have a bore larger than certain Continental armies because, whereas captured ammunition could be fired from English muskets, English leaden balls could not be fired out of theirs". The 1851 Minié was not the ideal choice of weapon for troops in combat. This can be seen from the many regimental reports which originated from trials carried out in August 1854. Here it was concluded that the barrel of this weapon was too hot to hold after firing between thirty to fifty rounds. Twelve to thirteen minutes had to be allowed for the weapon to cool sufficiently, raising fears that the powder might prematurely explode in the barrel causing injury. Furthermore, the Minié was over one pound heavier than the Enfield Pattern 1853, making it less than ideal to carry and handle.

The Duke of Wellington (1769–1852). It was not until after Wellington's death that "Ordnance" was able to introduce the smaller bore Enfield Rifle Pattern 1853. Wellington had argued that larger caliber ammunition was capable of bringing down a horse in battle by breaking its leg; he was of the opinion that smaller caliber rounds would pass straight through.

With the many logistical problems confronting the Army, ranging from the supply of equipment to suitability of weapons and ammunition, it would not seem unreasonable to question the competence of the Board of Ordnance and the military authorities. If they were unable to accomplish those tasks which were more suited to their military backgrounds, then it would be difficult to see how they could cope with technical matters concerning the design, manufacturing, and scheduling of weapons. Shipments of replacement arms from England were slow to arrive at the Crimea, this was primarily due to the problems already highlighted, ranging from the contract system and the strictness of view (quality control) to the failure of "Ordnance" to supply an adequate number of patterns and tools to the private gun trade which caused delays and further compromised weapon quality.

By 3rd January 1855, research has shown, there were contracts (not all signed) outstanding for up to 160,000 weapons, mainly the Enfield Pattern 1853. Although figures relating to the individual suppliers of weapons are not entirely clear, it can be deduced from the correspondence that orders for 100,000 guns had been placed with Birmingham contractors, 40,000 with Liège, 1,500 with London, and 1,000 with Enfield. "Ordnance" had promised that 10,000 of these arms would be delivered to Balaklava by the end of January, with a continuing schedule of 4,000 per month until May and each rifle was to be supplied with 500 cartridges. The grand plan was to have, by August or September, the Army in the Crimea, "entirely armed with rifles of one pattern - that of the 1853".

After all the complaints by "Ordnance" against the private gun trade, the above figures clearly show that they were the only sector of the arms industry capable of supplying reasonable quantities of weapons to the soldiers at the front, albeit behind schedule on occasion, and still by mainly labour-intensive methods of manufacture. However, as already pointed out, the delays were not entirely the fault of the private sector. Therefore, the establishment of the "Ordnance" factory at Enfield at the beginning of the century to secure adequate supplies of arms for the military without recourse to the private sector and the necessity of placing orders abroad, had clearly not achieved its goal. The successful lobbying of Parliament by the private gun trade had ensured that Enfield remained incapable of manufacturing large quantities of weapons. This had inadvertently brought foreign imports from Liège into the country when demand for arms increased. Here it might be argued that due to a failure by politicians to appreciate fully the technological requirements of a country with an empire to police, British interests abroad had been rendered vulnerable by the lack of a strategic weapon manufacturing policy.

Initially, it will be recalled, government had sought to develop a small arms strategy by setting up Enfield in 1816 but had bowed under political pressure from the private sector. However, in the early years, "Ordnance" had failed to heed George Lovell when he had suggested a sensible method of working with the gun trade, rather than in direct competition. No doubt a coordinated weapons manufacturing and development programme could have been advantageously cultivated between the private and public sectors based upon Lovell's recommendations. Failure of government to develop such a scheme in the relatively peaceful period after the Napoleonic conflict left Britain once again vulnerable when war loomed.

FAILURE OF GOVERNMENT TO LEARN FROM EXPERIENCE

When the British government decided to send a commission to America in 1854 to investigate the possible purchase of suitable arms-making machinery, the timing almost exactly coincided with Britain's entry into the Crimean War. Even after the commission had left England, Parliament was still arguing over the amounts of money to be spent on re-equipping the Enfield factory. In fact the initial sum was reduced from £30,000 to the absurd amount of £10,000 but was later reinstated, the commission being allowed an almost open-cheque facility to purchase the necessary machine tools. No doubt the outbreak of the Crimean conflict had persuaded Parliament to release its grip on the purse strings. By the lack of written evidence to the contrary, it would seem reasonable to conclude that "Ordnance" was not working toward a cohesive strategic plan for the British small arms industry with a view to securing future weapon supplies. Therefore, without the pressure created by the Crimean campaign it is unlikely that Enfield would have had the opportunity to become one of the world's leading small arms producers by the middle of the century. The episode would tend to reinforce the notion that the British government and its advisers lacked a fundamental knowledge of manufacturing matters, particularly an understanding of the planning processes and the timescales involved in preparing and equipping a small arms production plant. Although it has been suggested earlier that the private gun trade's influence upon Parliament had been exceedingly powerful, by which the trade had successfully resisted "Ordnance" intrusion into their industry, there is no evidence to suggest that government had the political will or commitment to become involved in full-scale small arms manufacture on its own account. Of course it might be argued that the long period of relative peace following the end of the Napoleonic Wars had lulled the British government into a false sense of security. If this was the case, then it would appear naive in the extreme, particularly if one remembers the vastness of the British Empire and the unpredictability of outbreaks of unrest. Under such circumstances one would have expected Britain to have been vigilant at all times, needing to be positioned to react quickly to restore law and order in any of her overseas possessions. Given such conditions, it would seem rational that Britain would require a plentiful supply of reliable arms to be called upon should such an emergency arise.

British and French troops relax at camp during the Crimean War.

The inside of a Redan (V-shaped battlefield defences) at the Crimean, after being abandoned by the Russians.

EVIDENCE OF "ORDNANCE" IGNORANCE

At a time when there was a desperate need to supply the Army at the Crimea with weapons of standard calibre and type, research at the National Archive has uncovered a substantial amount of correspondence between Captain Manly Dixon, Superintendent of the Enfield manufactory and a number of defence agencies relating to mounting pressure to introduce new weapon types. An undated letter from Dixon to "Ordnance" circa 30th May 1855, asked "whether it would be advisable to purchase 1,000 or 1,500 Sharpe's breech loading Carbines instead of issuing contracts for making the Victoria Carbine, a weapon which is all but useless". Dixon went on to suggest that the Sharpe's breech loader is "much superior to anything that has yet been invented" and he further pointed out that the Victoria Carbine "would take 6-7 months to manufacture". This figure would seem rather generous, as it will be recalled that just over a year before it had taken nine months to organise the production of only 286 of these weapons. In a reply from "Ordnance" to Dixon dated 5th June it was stated that Viscount Hardinge had inspected a Sharpe's breech loader and "considers a Carbine invented by Mr Prince to

A piper of the 42nd Highlanders, the Black Watch, at the Crimean.

be superior". He also went on to suggest that "some of Prince's pattern be made and distributed for test to the Regiments with the Sharpe's". In the mean-time, Dixon received an order for 4,000 Victoria Carbines to be delivered to General Beatson for the Irregular Turkish Cavalry. Dixon's reply exudes frustration when he states "there are no contracts for material for these arms, at present existing and there are no materials in store". Later in his letter he forcefully concluded "The question now is whether a contract shall issue for an arm for Cavalry purposes which hardly shoots straight at 100 yards, is cumbrous, and difficult to load on horseback and requires a different ammunition to any other arm in the British Army".

Viscount Henry Hardinge (1785–1856), Master General of Ordnance during the most critical period of small arms procurement during the Crimean War.

This is a damning report by any account and is further evidence of how critical the arms supply situation had become. Not only is it an indication of the plight of the frontline troops, but it illustrates the failure of "Ordnance" to recognise or understand the basic requirements of the small arms industry and the timescales involved in implementing a new manufacturing programme. This latter point should have appeared particularly pertinent to Hardinge, particularly after Dixon had already explained in previous correspondence that the Victoria Carbine, a weapon which had already been in production "would take 6-7 months to manufacture". For Hardinge to propose that an entirely new weapon be manufactured and "distributed for test to the Regiments" would suggest not only that Dixon's former point had been missed or ignored but also that he was prepared to carry out experiments with an untried arm in time of war. This latter fact seems quite extraordinary and almost beyond belief, again emphasising that the military side of "Ordnance" had little idea of timescales and were seemingly prepared to risk soldier's lives while they were trying to find an improved weapon. In a further communication between "Ordnance" and Dixon it is suggested that "Viscount Hardinge is now of the opinion that Mr Leitch breech loading Carbine be examined". From the correspondence it would appear that this weapon was being recommended for use with the British Cavalry. Dixon therefore suggests as an expedient that Colt's revolvers should be issued to the Cavalry in lieu of the Victoria Carbine. It will be recalled that Dixon had been highly critical of this latter weapon and, apart from it being an old design, there were no gun stocks available.

In a letter to Dixon from the War Department dated 11th July 1855 it was stated that Hardinge had now "re-considered his opinion and understands that the breech loader would be for the Cavalry only". Dixon was also informed that Hardinge did not want the Sharpe's or Colt's weapons purchased from America and he was given the news that a Leitch breech loader was being sent to him for evaluation after the weapon had already been examined by a Board of Cavalry Officers who apparently found it "excellent practice at 300 yards". This communication was followed by another letter dated 8th August, informing Dixon that Hardinge had "decided the best fire arm for the Cavalry is Leitch's breech loading rifle". The message went on to say "this improved arm will of course do away with the necessity of anymore Victoria Carbines being procured". By 15th August Dixon was replying in very strong terms in relation to his findings on the Leitch rifle. Dixon explained that Mr Leitch had been given the opportunity to fire his weapon at Enfield, "a model which he [Leitch] stated had been shewn to the Board of Cavalry Officers and approved by them and subsequently approved and inspected by Viscount Hardinge". The opportunity was taken by Dixon to report on how the rifle performed in the demonstration given by Mr Leitch, stating; "The results showed that in our opinion the arm is less adapted for Cavalry purposes than any other which has been submitted". These views were also supported by Captain Warlow, an experienced "Ordnance" officer and one of the members of the 1854 commission to America. Warlow found up to six areas of complaint with the weapon. These and Dixon's opinions received the support and backing of James Gunner, Storekeeper at Enfield. A communication to Dixon from "Ordnance" dated 15th August informed him that Hardinge:

> recommends that instructions be immediately given for the preparation of 15,000 of Leitch's breech loading rifled carbines in order that a sufficient reserve be at hand to meet casualties. His Lordship would be glad to learn how soon any, and what proportion of these weapons may be expected to be ready in order that the Regiments serving in the Crimea may be supplied at the earliest possible period.

As the date of Hardinge's instruction coincided with that of Dixon's report on the Leitch rifle, it is not obvious from the correspondence whether the former communication arrived at Enfield before or after the technical assessment took place. If it came before, this would indicate that the Board had already made up its mind and was therefore not prepared to receive a serious evaluation of the weapon by Enfield personnel. Had it come after, it would imply a large measure of arrogance on behalf of the Board, particularly as the technical advice had come from three of the country's leading experts on military small arms. Had Enfield not possessed men of the calibre of Dixon and his colleagues who understood not only the intricacies of production and procurement timescales but military requirements as well, and were also prepared to stand their ground and argue their case with high ranking "Ordnance" officers, it is difficult to contemplate what fate might have eventually befallen the British soldier. However, the whole episode and particularly the action of ordering Dixon to produce 15,000 Leitch breech loaders, illustrates the Master General's lack of manufacturing knowledge. This clearly demonstrates that Hardinge had no idea of how long it would take to tool-up and prepare for manufacture.

A *Punch* cartoon depicting British forces ignoring a bombardment by cannon during the Crimean War. The artist no doubt wished to convey an impression of British nonchalance to the readers back home.

EXPLANATIONS FOR "ORDNANCE" INCOMPETENCE EMERGE

It should be recognised that the dialogue between Captain Dixon and in particular Viscount Henry Hardinge has been truncated for brevity. However, analysing the correspondence and noting the critical period during which the exchange took place has provided a fresh insight into behind-the-scenes actions of senior military and Board of Ordnance personnel.The investigation has helped uncover what is sometimes perceived as the mysteries surrounding certain aspects of military decision making, the results of which are often viewed with incredulity.Those outside the process who question the reasons, which on occasion appear irrational, can begin to understand why certain actions were or were not taken. Historians researching the transfer of the "American system of manufactures" to Britain have failed to explore fully the Board of Ordnance comprehension of military supply chain requirements, particularly at the time of the Crimean War. Now, by opening this line of enquiry it has been possible to demonstrate that certain military and Board of Ordnance officers, with responsibility for supplying small arms to frontline troops, lacked a fundamental understanding of the weapon manufacturing process and consequently the ability to appreciate development and delivery timescales. The correspondence has shown quite clearly that there was considerable antagonism between the technical experts at Enfield, the military and "Ordnance" bureaucrats, further demonstrating that this latter group were not versed in a basic understanding of the problems caused by re-scheduling or re-planning production.

Lord Raglan (1788–1855), Commander in Chief of the British Army at the Crimean. Raglan was blamed for the poor communication that tragically caused the Light Brigade to be ordered to charge the Russian guns at Balaklava. The event has been immortalized in the poem "The Charge of the Light Brigade" by Alfred Lord Tennyson.

Neither had the importance of maintaining long-term manufacturing stability through continuity of product design been grasped. It would also appear that the Board had little comprehension of the limitations of the gauges, tools and machinery which had been ordered from America to equip the Enfield factory. This equipment had been specifically designed to support large-scale manufacture of one particular weapon, the Pattern 1853 rifle, and could not be expected to support any other

A painting of Lord Raglan's funeral cortege. He died ten days after the Light Brigade's tragic charge on the Russian guns.

pattern of arm. Perhaps the problems of a nineteenth century manufacturing-ignorant government bureaucracy were best summed up by G.R. Searle when he wrote:

> the most important administrative appointments soon became the preserve of "gentlemen" who had benefited from a "liberal" university education, but who possessed neither practical experience nor knowledge relevant to their work. Yet partly because of the assumption that specialists were spendthrifts who needed tight curbing, public officials with technical qualification and attainments usually found themselves subordinated at all points to these "general administrators".

Of course, the lack of understanding by the Board and other military personnel may have been a question of poor communication by engineers; but this argument can generally be discounted on the grounds that there had been almost forty years of relative peace for good liaisons to have developed, had there been the will. Views of engineers had been expressed and recorded, some by famous and high-profile men like Whitworth, Nasmyth and Anderson, when they drew up reports for government agencies and gave evidence before the various select committees, so it was not as if information concerning engineering and manufacturing matters was unknown in high places. The lack of "Ordnance" understanding can again be seen after the adoption of the Enfield Pattern 1853 rifle as the standard arm for the forces in the Crimea. It was hoped that the delivery of this weapon in quantity to the frontline troops would overcome the potentially disastrous situation of having more than one type of ammunition in circulation. As pointed out earlier, problems had already been caused for the Army with the issue of a least three different calibre weapons to the front. However, from the correspondence between Dixon and Hardinge, it can be seen that the Board and influential military officers were changing their minds almost daily, encouraging Enfield to introduce new weapon types, some of which, if accepted, would have required additional designs of ammunition and training of the men, hardly a situation to be contemplated when war was raging. While these distracting communications between "Ordnance" and Enfield were taking place, it should be remembered that substantial contracts had been placed with the private sector for the Pattern 1853 and shipments of the weapon to the Army were already underway.

Investigating the correspondence between "Ordnance" and Enfield has helped to clarify the reasons governing the timing of the British government's intervention into the traditional small arms manufacturing business of the private sector, bringing about for the first time the entry of "Ordnance" into large-scale military weapon manufacture. In fact it is the clarification of the timing issue which has provided important information, showing how Enfield was catapulted into adopting revolutionary methods of mass production with new imported machine tools, rather than having a more sedate and evolutionary approach to large-scale arms manufacture. Had the Crimean conflict not come about, then Enfield may well have retained its original role as a small-scale manufacturing unit with responsibilities for weapon repair, research and development.

PLAYING A DANGEROUS GAME?

Early in 1855, work on the new buildings began at Enfield to house the machinery on order from America, the task of construction being undertaken by the Royal Engineers under the command of Major General Collinson. While preparation for the site's expansion was taking place, a decision to alter dramatically the terms and conditions of the workforce was implemented. A memorandum dated 4th July 1855 explained that the current terms and conditions of workmen employed by the "Ordnance" establishment at Enfield would be suspended as of the 21st "when they will be considered as ceasing to belong to the factory – as it is hoped that many will be willing to re-engage under the new system". The new arrangements required "old hands to be pensioned", and it was proposed that workmen "such as receive it [the pension] for long and faithful services shall be recommended for a gratuity". Furthermore, an abstract of the rules was to be hung in the factory telling the workforce that they would have to apply to the Superintendent before the 17th July to be re-engaged. The working hours were to be brought into line with other private factories in Britain: 10.5 hours per day for the first five days and 7 hours on the sixth, bringing the total working week to 59.5 hours. Even senior craftsmen did not escape the changes. All Superintendent Armourers were informed that, on the 23rd of July, they would receive their instructions from the Tower "under the immediate superintendence of Mr Phillcox but subject to the order and charge of Mr Turner". Time keeping was to be formally structured, gates to be opened at 5.45 a.m., work commencing at 6 a.m. Workmen arriving five minutes late would be deducted 15-minutes' pay; arrival after 6.15 a.m. would see 30-minutes' pay deducted. Gates were to be closed at 6.30 a.m. and workmen arriving after this time would have to wait until the breakfast break at 9 a.m. to be allowed in. There was to be a time book which would show the punctuality or lateness of the employees and this would be reflected in the amount of wages received by individuals. Wages would be paid before the Saturday dinner break.

From the timing of the new working practices it would seem that management had taken a terrible risk. The act of introducing these fresh terms and conditions could have easily provoked a serious strike. With Britain deeply involved in the Crimean War, further problems with the supply of arms would seem to have been the last thing government wanted. It was probable, however, that "Ordnance" felt confident in taking this action, perhaps banking on the knowledge that memories of the 1852 "great lock out" were still fresh in workers' minds. The risk of industrial action may also have appeared slight because, as the Enfield factory was a government establishment, the workers enjoyed better terms and conditions than their private-sector counterparts. From the rapidly rising output of the Enfield factory after January 1857, it would seem fair to conclude that the changes went through relatively smoothly.

BIRTH OF THE UNION

With the organisational changes taking place, it is probably no coincidence that on the 5th November 1855 the Amalgamated Society of Engineers (ASE) formed the Enfield Lock Branch. The inaugural meeting was attended by the Union's General Secretary, William Allan, who formally declared the Branch open. Unfortunately the Union minute books for this important period in the birth of the Branch are incomplete and the early entries are erratic. For example, the second entry does not occur until 24th February 1857, the business being conducted is of a general administrative nature and sadly does not refer to the introduction of the new American machine tools at the Enfield factory.

A parade of delivery carts, August 1897, to celebrate the 25th anniversary of the founding of the Enfield Highway Co-operative Society. The Society had originally been the initiative of the workforce of the Royal Small Arms Factory at Enfield Lock and the Assistant Superintendent, Major Dyer, in 1872.

The emblem of the Amalgamated Society of Engineers, Machinists, Millwrights, Smiths and Pattern Makers; the Amalgamated Society of Engineers (ASE). On 5th November 1855 the Enfield Lock Branch was formed. The inaugural meeting was attended by the ASE General Secretary, William Allen, who formally declared the Branch open.

From an examination of later entries in the minute books, it can clearly be established that the Branch was catering strictly for skilled craftsmen only. This applied not only to members serving the necessary time appropriate to their trade but also to discrimination against men with physical disabilities. Membership of able-bodied men was actively encouraged as this was thought necessary to maintaining high standards of craftsmanship. At the time, skilled workers' jobs were under threat from the increasing number of machine tools being introduced into the Enfield factory. The following examples taken from the minutes give a clear indication of the measure of strictness being operated by the Branch in an effort to preserve and maintain a skilled membership:

> October 26th 1872 - That the sympathy of this Branch be conveyed to Mr Tuckey on his being disqualified to becoming a member of this Society through his loss of two fingers on one hand.

> January 17th 1874 – That Thomas Tanner be admitted a member of this Society. He having undergone an examination by Doctor J. Hutchinson of the Ophthalmic Hospital, London, who certifies that his left eye is perfect, and that the right eye suffers from a congenital defect and that it will not be detrimental to his following his employment.
>
> January 31st 1874 – That our Secretary be instructed to write to the Council to know whether we are justified in admitting a member suffering from a rupture to the sick benefit of our Society.
>
> October 10th 1874 – That our Secretary be requested to write to Newcastle informing the Secretary that James Trigg was not working at this Factory as a mechanic he being employed while working here on the component parts of the gun.

On reading these extracts one is left with the impression that a type of craft elitism was being operated. This may have accounted for the relatively small number of men belonging to the Branch. In 1855 the Branch membership was only 44, rising to 122 by 1880. The workforce estimates of the RSAF Superintendent and historian G.H. Roberts suggest that in 1858 "about 1,000 unskilled or semi-skilled and 250 men were employed, a considerable number of whom had come from Col. S. Colt's Factory at Pimlico". Therefore, during the early years of the Branch, membership as a proportion of workers employed at the factory was less than four percent.

A CLIMATE OF MIXED VIEWS AND UNCERTAINTY

After almost forty years of only partial manufacturing involvement, government had been forced by war to accept responsibility for the full-scale production of military small arms. However, the plan to expand Enfield was not shared by all politicians, some taking the view that a government-owned armoury was not essential, believing that the private gun trade could provide all of Britain's military requirements without placing an undue burden on the Exchequer. Research has shown that, if "Ordnance" had sought to establish sensible long-term contracts with the private sector and taken the trouble to foster good relationships with the gun makers, supplying them with reasonable quantities of patterns and gauges, a reliable source of military weapons could have been developed with minimum reliance upon public expenditure.

The report of the Select Committee on Small Arms, 1854, was able to present an objective analysis of the problems befalling the gun trade in the supply and manufacture of military weapons. In drawing up their report the committee reached the following conclusions:

> While Your Committee recommended the system of contracting for the supply of Small Arms should not be discontinued, they are, nevertheless, of opinion that a manufactory of Small Arms under the Board of Ordnance should be tried to a limited extent. This manufactory would serve as an experiment of the advantages to be derived from the more extensive application of machinery, as a check upon the price of contractors, and as a resource in times of emergency, and it should be arranged with a view to its economical working.

While it is clear that the committee wanted to retain the contract system and had not wished to give Enfield sole responsibility for the production of all military small arms, their recommendation had nevertheless allowed "Ordnance" the opportunity to keep their feet firmly in the manufacturing door. When Britain joined the conflict in the Crimea, followed by the purchase of machine tools from America, the chance for "Ordnance" to push the door fully open finally came.

It would seem unreasonable to assume that politicians were unaware of the high levels of expenditure required to fund a fully mechanised modern small arms factory on a continuous basis. Apart from the financial information coming before the various select committees, there were also the examples of factories directly under "Ordnance" control, like Woolwich Arsenal and Waltham Abbey Gunpowder Mills. Furthermore, from the haphazard and intermittent working of the contract system, it should have been obvious to politicians that there were no individual manufacturers outside of government who were big enough to have the confidence, let alone the finances, to risk investment in a large-scale manufacturing plant. Many private companies had yet to be convinced of the superiority of the "American system of manufactures" over the traditional labour-intensive methods of gun production. This latter system had generally served them well over the years, allowing the private sector the flexibility to exploit different markets at minimum capital outlay.

POLITICS SLOW ENGINEERING INFLUENCE

It was not only politicians who had appeared to lack the imagination and understanding of the needs of their armed forces at a time of a rapidly changing technology. After all, many were under pressure from their gun-making constituents. The collective responsibility of the Board of Ordnance was also found wanting. They had allowed the British Army to embark for the Crimea with inadequate and out-of-date weapons. Moreover, as research has shown, even the Master General was prepared to continue a time-consuming and unhelpful dialogue with the technical and manufacturing experts over the introduction and trial of new weapons.This not only demonstrates a lack of understanding of the planning required in the manufacturing process but also an ignorance of the problems which would have undoubtedly been caused by issuing unfamiliar weapons to soldiers at the front (or perhaps it was naivety). Placing untried battlefield weapons in the hands of men in action, who had not been give the opportunity to train with them, would have no doubt resulted in disastrous consequences, not to mention confusion if new types of ammunition had to be issued as well.

The lack of "Ordnance" understanding of manufacturing issues would suggest that by the middle of the nineteenth century the voices of the engineers and technicians, although beginning to gain respect, had yet to be allowed to influence the decision-making process. Perhaps Viscount Hardinge was still stirred by his earlier experiences of the former Inspector of Small Arms, George Lovell, of whom he had expressed the view (possibly unfairly) that "The Inspector has an undue confidence in his own authority to act independent of the Board or of my own authority...".

The timing of the expansion and equipping of the Enfield factory when the Crimean War was in progress demonstrates clearly how unprepared the Board of Ordnance were for major conflict. In fact the situation was even worse than it appears on the surface. A report, called for by John Anderson, Inspector of Machinery and published in 1857, suggests that the new factory to house the machinery from America was originally planned for Woolwich. It was not until 2nd February 1855 (after Anderson's return from the United States) that the Board of Ordnance gave the order to commence building on the Enfield site. Naturally this caused further delays as plans had to be redrawn and the work put out to tender. The building was completed in 1856 but not before more costly delays were encountered due to "the ground being a bog of peat".

As it has been shown, the whole episode surrounding government small arms production in the early to mid-1850s is one of general indecision, confusion and "Ordnance" incompetence. This would seem to be an extremely serious state of affairs for the British nation to be placed in, particularly when considering the developing international scene. It was not as if politicians had suddenly realised that if Russia were to occupy Turkey, then India, the jewel in the British crown, would suddenly become exceedingly vulnerable.

Russia had been expanding her empire for years and there was more than enough intelligence information from British agents to have caused politicians considerable anxiety. More than ever, the British government needed an arms manufacturing strategy which would introduce stability to the supply of weapons to her troops. Would the incoming "American system", developed by engineers, based on new production and assembly principles, achieve this?

TIME FOR CHANGE

The arrival of the "American system of manufactures" (as it later became known) in Britain was to show, by the early 1860s, that Enfield was in a position to influence dramatically and change totally the method of British small arms production. At the time it was probably not fully appreciated how this new system of manufacture might affect other industries in Britain. The change appears to have been influential on at least two levels. First, the publicity given to Enfield had made the factory highly visible. This had set other industrialists thinking and they began considering the installation of new plant and equipment. Secondly, the new factory processes had imposed different standards on contractors which by the 1860s meant external supplies of military arms would only be accepted by "Ordnance" if made with interchangeable parts. This caused suppliers like the London Gun Company and the amalgamation of Birmingham gun makers, by 1861 called BSA, to implement machine-intensive production.

Although not referring directly to Enfield, Clive Treblicock wrote in relation to his "spin-off" theory, "The intricacy of the new weapons, the excellence of the manufacturing equipment, the heavy commitment to research - as well as the advocacy of the trade journal - would strongly suggest that by the 1880s the British armament industry had reached a level of technical achievement from which it could profitably influence 'civilian' industries". Free of pressure from the private gun trade and without the need to play political games with the contractors, Enfield's role had changed from a small-volume repair shop to that of a major international small arms manufacturer. By 1860 the annual production figure for rifles alone had reached 90,707 - 1,744 per week.

ENFIELD'S GROWING FAME

A visible consequence of the Enfield factory, after full-scale production commenced in January 1857 with the imported American machine tools, was the vast amount of attention it attracted, particularly from the national press. Articles appeared in newspapers and learned journals proclaiming admiration for the manufacturing system and extolling the "beauty" of the machinery installed at the plant. The reporting in some instances exuded such national pride that the reader might be forgiven for believing mistakenly that the factory and its equipment was a marvellous piece of solely British ingenuity. Being cynical, it could be argued that this was the government encouraging publicity for the factory as a way of justifying to the public the large amount of capital expenditure, rather than simply being a piece of Victorian pride. In the period immediately following the cessation of hostilities in the Crimea much publicity was given to the new factory highlighting its modern production techniques and machine tools. Although several articles paid tribute to American machine manufacturers Robbins & Lawrence and the Ames Company, the references were often glossed over as in the case of *The Mechanic's Magazine* of 23rd August 1861. The machinery designers are referred to as "our American cousins", implying that the writer was trying to claim credit for Britain through a family connection. The fame of the Enfield factory was not short lived, neither were the admirers confined to the world of adults.

No doubt wishing to encourage the younger generation and perhaps to secure the craftsmen of the future, the *Boy's Own Magazine* ran an article in 1860 entitled "Manly Exercises, Rifles and Rifle Shooting" which gave an account of weapon manufacture at Enfield. The writer, obviously overwhelmed by the experience of his visit to the factory, described the large machine room in the following florid terms:

> Let our readers imagine, if they can, a single room more than an acre in extent, lofty, and well lit, in which some thousand men and boys are increasingly employed in superintending machinery. The ear is pained by the hum of fly-wheels, which revolve in thousands till the eye is giddy with their whirl. Miles of shafting are spinning round mistily, with a monotonous hum; the room is almost darkened, and the view completely obscured, by some 50,000 or 60,000 feet of broad, flapping lathe-bands, which are driving no less than 600 distinct machines, all going together, on their own allotted tasks, with a tremulous rapidity and ease that seems to swallow up the work like magic, and the first sight of which is inexpressibly astonishing to the spectator. It takes some minutes before the visitor can subdue the overwhelming feeling of surprise which this scene of activity always excites, no matter how often entered on.

John Anderson, the engineer from Woolwich Arsenal who had been a member of the 1854 three-man commission to America, gave lectures to the Institute of Mechanical Engineers. In 1858 he read a paper in Newcastle on the applications of the "Copying or Transfer Principle in the Production of Wooden Articles" in which he described the sequenced operation of the new gun-stock forming machinery at Enfield. A further paper in 1862 on the "Copying Principle in the Manufacture and Rifling of Guns" was given in Birmingham. Here Anderson described the levels of precision attained in machining and measurement at the government ordnance factories at Woolwich and Enfield. At the end of the lecture the chairman remarked that members would have an opportunity of visiting "the works at Woolwich and seeing the whole of the processes described in the paper in the manufacture and rifling of guns; and also of visiting the Small Arms Factory at Enfield, where the same principles had been carried out by Mr. Anderson, and the same accuracy of workmanship attained". While Enfield was enjoying the attention and prestige of a modern, state-of-the-art factory, there were remarks from members of Anderson's audience which suggested that Britain's manufacturing industries were suffering from under-investment. A Mr. Richardson, who had previously visited the Woolwich factory, commented "It would be a great advantage if the engineering workshops throughout the country would endeavour to approach to the same amount of perfection, by employing a better class of machinery and tools, which would produce an important advance in mechanical engineering".

The increased productivity brought about by the introduction of the new machine tools coupled with the technology of interchangeability, gave Enfield a reputation as a centre of excellence. This point was emphasised by Howard Blackmore when he quoted William Greener the respected quality gun maker, a man apparently not given to generous comment, although he said of the factory "Enfield, the seat of the government manufacture of small arms, will become a celebrated place in future history; its productions being now one of the wonders of the present age". Greener's view supports the notion that Enfield was seen more in terms of making a contribution towards production technology rather than having a role as a small arms design centre. In 1866 "Ordnance", now the War Office, introduced the system of open competition as a means to acquire new weapons. Private inventors were invited to submit their designs which would be evaluated under nine performance headings. Here accuracy of fire was listed first and, perhaps not surprisingly, manufacturing last. This now gave Enfield an additional role above that of a weapons manufacture, making the plant more of a trial judge and weapon modifier rather than having the responsibility of a design house.

THE MESSAGE SPREADS TO THE PRIVATE SECTOR

With the repeated enthusiastic coverage given to the Enfield factory by journalists and others, and the influencing of engineers and entrepreneurs through lectures within learned societies, the conditions were building up for a watershed within the British gun trade. Continually suffering shortages of skilled labour, yet encouraged by the sudden demand for arms brought about by the outbreak of war in the Crimea and later by the American Civil War in 1861, it had become clear to the private gun trade that if it wished to secure future orders for military weapons, manufacturing methods within its industry would have to change dramatically. No longer could the private sector expect to enjoy the same monopolistic conditions which prevailed prior to 1854 and which had effectively denied "Ordnance" the ability to compete for military small arms contracts. Now the private gun trade would have to compete with the much publicised and highly visible government factory at Enfield which was now able to dictate even stricter terms on which "Ordnance" would accept weapons and parts. In future, weapons would only be accepted if they conformed to a precise standard and were manufactured with interchangeable parts. For generations the private gunsmiths had operated within a system of small shops employing mainly hand skills. If the private industry was to survive late into the nineteenth century and beyond, it would need to alter dramatically its method of production. The gauntlet had been thrown down by Enfield and the private gun trade was about to pick it up and accept the challenge by altering its method of manufacturing military weapons.

In 1861, four years after the RSAF commenced full-scale production with the imported machinery from America using the techniques of interchangeability, a group of midland firms came together to erect a new small arms factory at Small Heath in Birmingham. The plant was similar to the installation at Enfield and purpose built, modelling itself on the "American system" using the techniques of interchangeable production. Over the coming years, the conglomerate known as the Birmingham Small Arms Company (BSA) would demonstrate how the lessons learned from the manufacturc of standardised weapons could be transferred to the mass production of consumer products such as the bicycle.

Perhaps the most significant change for the private sector came from a complete reversal of government policy which moved from a position of obstruction and arm's-length dealing to one of close cooperation. Instead of withholding patterns and gauges as they had in the past, Enfield was actively encouraged to assist BSA in

After considerable investment at Enfield Lock in a failed attempt to produce small arms for the Crimean War, the new factory finally began large-scale production by January 1857. The opportunity to off-load some of the stock came with the commencement of the American Civil War in 1861 when Enfield supplied large numbers of the Enfield Rifle Pattern 1853 to both the armies of the North and South.

making weapons which were compatible with their own production and therefore interchangeable between factories. The following statement by a grateful Birmingham Small Arms Company shows just how far "Ordnance" had moved from its earlier position:

> Every assistance has been rendered to the directors by the War Dept. of H.M. Government. The experience of Enfield has been freely placed at their disposal; free access has been granted to the Royal Manufactory with permission to make drawings of machinery. Models and gauges have been supplied which have effected for the company an incalculable saving.

This was a far cry from the denial of the means of measurement which had occurred during Lovell's time as Inspector of Small Arms.

GOVERNMENT ENCOURAGES INDUSTRIAL INVESTMENT

Although it is true that BSA took delivery of specialist gun-stocking machines from the Ames Manufacturing Company of Chicopee,

Massachusetts similar to those supplied to Enfield, the pattern of machine tool acquisition was beginning to change. Roger Lumley has concluded from his research that claims suggesting the majority of the early machinery installed at BSA had come from the United States of America were false. During the 1860s, out of a total of 430 machine tools purchased, only 65 came from the U.S.A., the original order for American equipment being cancelled at the outbreak of the Civil War of 1861. Of the 2,324 machines purchased by BSA in the nineteenth century, less than seven percent came from abroad. The Leeds-based company Greenwood and Batley, which was only founded in 1856, was rapidly becoming recognised both at home and abroad as a quality producer of machine tools for the manufacture of small arms. Prior to supplying BSA this manufacturer had already equipped the London Armoury Company at Bow, giving it an output capacity capable of reaching 900 complete arms per week. So in a way the machine-tool story relating to self-acting mass-production methods had come full circle: the ideas had transferred to America from Portsmouth and elsewhere at the beginning of the century; returned to Enfield by the middle at an advanced state of development; finally to be taken up by British machine-tool manufacturers, who subsequently spread the technology both within Britain and abroad. Ironically and by default, the British government, by its ability to place large orders for small arms, had broken the mould of the private sector's small-workshop culture, forcing investment in capital equipment through the formation of larger manufacturing units. Looking from the position of the twenty-first century, it can be seen that the act of importing specialised machine tools from America was an extremely influential component in a cocktail of many ingredients which helped to shape British light engineering. Although the introduction of the machine tool into the small arms industry influenced the spread of mass production technology in Britain, which eventually transferred to other industries and encouraged greater size, it also had the effect of reducing the ability of industry to be flexible, thereby limiting the individuality of the product. Therefore, standardisation of parts became to mean standardisation of product.

REFERENCES

Anderson, John, "On the Application of the Copying Principle in The Manufacture and Rifling of Guns", Paper given before The Institute of Mechanical Engineers Proceedings 1862, published by the Institution, Birmingham 1862, pp.125-45.

AUEW District Office, Edmonton, London, *Minute Book of the Enfield Lock Branch - ASE 1855-1865,* (First minute book). "See also, The First 80 Years,

Some Account To 1935 of the Enfield Lock Branch (founded 1855) of the Amalgamated Union of Engineers and Foundry Workers, Formerly the A.E.U. Originally the A.S.E." p.4.

Bailey, De Witt, "George Lovell And The Growth Of The RSAF Enfield", Paper presented at MA Day School, Middlesex University, 4th July 1992, p.8.

Blackmore, Howard L., "Military Gun Manufacturing In London and the Adoption of Interchangeability", *Arms Collecting*, Vol. 29, No. 4, November 1991, p.121.

Boy's Own Magazine, "Manly Exercises, Rifle and Rifle Shooting", Vol. 6, 1860.

The Engineer, "Birmingham Small Arms Factory", Vol. 16, 25th December 1863, p.375.

Gleason, F.W. Foster, "Arms For Men", Ordnance, July/August 1961, p.62.

Holt, Elizabeth, *The Crimean War*, Wayland Publishers, London, 1974, pp.117–19

House of Lords Record Office, London, "Report from the Select Committee on Small Arms," 12th May 1854, Reports Committee's Vol. XVIII-1854, p.257.

House of Lords Record Office, London, "Report of the Committee on the Machinery of the United States of America, Presented to the House of Commons in Pursuance of their Address, 10th July, 1855", pp.543–4.

Kirby, Charles, "Service Rifle SNAFU", *Handgunner*, No. 34, June 1986, pp.19–22. The article gives a classic illustration of how confusion between a government manufacturing plant (RSAF) and a government body (MOD), over the alleged accidental firing of the SA80 when dropped, caused production delays by bureaucrats insisting on modifications to the weapon which were probably unnecessary.

Lumley, Roger, "The American System of Manufacturers in Birmingham: Production Methods at the Birmingham Small Arms Co. in the Nineteenth Century", *Business History*, Vol. 31, 1989, p.37.

Mechanics Magazine, "The Enfield Small Arms Factory", Leviathan Workshops. No 11, 23rd August 1861, pp.110–11.

Ministry of Defence Pattern Room, Nottingham (archive now located at the library of the Royal Armouries, Leeds), Roberts, G.H., CBE M.INST. C.E. (Superintendent RSAF 1922–31), "Notes on The History of the Royal Small Arms Factory, Enfield Lock", unsigned typed manuscript circa 1931, p.10.

National Archive, Kew, "Telegraph Information Crimea, 1854", reference WO 33/2A.

National Archive, Kew, "Report, August 1854, concerning trials by different regiments regarding 1851 Mini", reference WO 44/701.

National Archive, Kew, correspondence between Lt. Colonel Griffiths, Mr J. Wood, "Ordnance and War Department, 1854–1855", reference WO 44/701.

[It is worth noting, that the closeness of the dates on this correspondence – that is to say, sent 25th April, note on back 26th April – suggest that the message had been telegraphed. As a point of information, there was in fact considerable telegraph activity at the Crimea. The Gateshead firm of Newell & Company took part in laying a marine cable under the

Bosphorus and the French had established a link to Paris. This therefore corrects the statement of the American Historian, F.W. Foster Gleason, when he suggested that the Civil War of 1861 was the "first telegraph war".]

National Archive, Kew, "Correspondence between Captain Dixon, Ordnance and War Department, 1854-1855", reference WO 44/701.

National Archive, Kew, Circular, 27th January 1855, reference WO 44/701.

The Victoria carbine had a calibre of 0.733in., the Minié 0.753in. and the Enfield Pattern 1853 0.577in.

National Archive, Kew, Ten Page Memorandum, 3rd January 1855, Correspondence, 2nd March 1855, 10th March 1855, 31st March 1855, reference WO 44/701.

National Archive, Kew, Memorandum 4th July 1855, Work Rules - RSAF, reference WO 44/701.

National Archive, Kew, "General Statement of the Past and Present Condition of the Several Manufacturing Branches of the War Department, as called for by a letter dated 8th May 1856 by John Anderson, Inspector of Machinery", reference WO44/701.

Reynolds, E.G.B., "Early Enfield Arms - The Muzzle Loaders", *Small Arms Profile* No. 14, pp.26-7.

Richards, D.S., *The Savage Frontier, A history of the Anglo-Afghan Wars*, Macmillan, London, 1990, pp.1-16.

Searle, G.R., *The Quest for National Efficiency*, Basil Blackwell, Oxford, 1971, p.21.

Treblicock, Clive, "'Spin-Off in British Economic History', Armaments and Industry 1760-1914", *Economic History Review*, 2nd Ser. XX11, 1969, p.481.

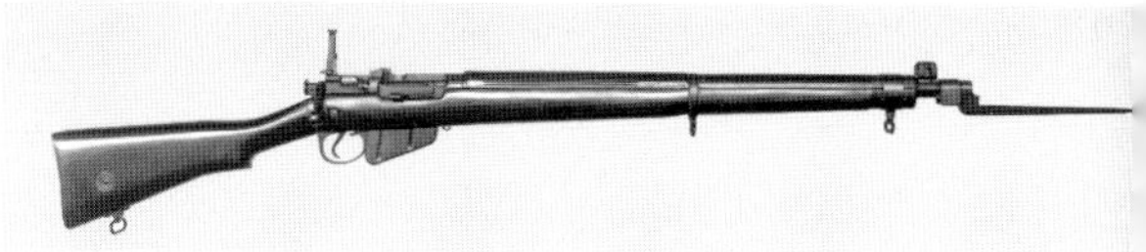

4. WHO PUT THE LEE IN THE "LEE-ENFIELD RIFLE"?

If you were to ask the average citizen of Enfield what made the town famous, the probable answer would be the Lee-Enfield Rifle. While it is true that the Pattern 1853 series rifle was the first British weapon to have the distinction of being named after a town (Enfield), the name Lee did not arrive on the scene until much later in the century and had nothing to do with either the river or the valley.

The Pattern 1853, a muzzle loader, first saw service with the British Army in the Crimean War (1853–1856) but did not go into full-scale production until January 1857. Muzzle loaders had distinct disadvantages for the soldier in the heat of battle as the ball and charge had to be rammed down the barrel with a rod (ramrod). This meant it was necessary for the soldier to stand upright to accomplish the task, presenting the enemy with a simple target.

By the 1860s, muzzle loading had become old technology as the method of breech loading increased in popularity. However, there were substantial stocks of the Enfield Pattern 1853 held by the British Army after the Crimean War and it made economic sense to have them converted to the new Snider breech loading system. Apart from the improved way of loading, the Snider had also been designed to accept the revolutionary rolled brass cartridge

Lee Enfield Rifles, 0.303" SMLE (Mk. III)

Lee Enfield Rifle No. 4 (Mk. I) with short bayonet No. 2 (Mk. 1)

developed by Colonel Boxer at Woolwich. Now it was possible for the soldier to load his weapon with comparative ease and safety, while lying prone on the ground.

The decision to use Snider's method of converting the Pattern 1853 had been arrived at through open competition. In August 1864, following the recommendations of the Committee on Breech Loading Arms, the War Office issued an advertisement inviting gun makers and inventors to submit plans to convert the Enfield Pattern 1853 from a muzzle loader to a breech loader, calling for two main criteria to be met. Firstly, the cost was "not to exceed £1 per arm" and secondly it was a requirement that "The shooting of the converted arm [should] not be inferior to the Enfield rifle" (unmodified muzzle loader). On completion of the modifications the weapons were to be assessed for accuracy, penetration, initial velocity, recoil, rapidity of fire, liability to failure, simplicity of management, fouling and exposure to weather.

The advertisement attracted fifty different applicants for the work, which after careful examination were whittled down to the eight most promising candidates. Over the coming months, extensive trials were carried out when it was reported that more than 5,500 rounds were fired with only one mis-fire. This not only gave the committee faith in the breech-loading system, but also the confidence to recommend the Snider method of conversion.

Over the years, the improved weapon was to go through a long evolutionary process of development when different inventors' systems were tried – Martini-Henry, Enfield-Martini, Lee-Burton, Lee-Metford, to name but a few. However, great emphasis was placed by the War Office upon having a design which would always function reliably under the severest of battlefield conditions (exposure to weather and mud). In 1895, the forerunner of the weapon which was to serve the Allied Forces throughout two world wars and beyond eventually emerged. This was the highly acclaimed Lee-Enfield Magazine Rifle Mk. 1. But what about the connection with the name Lee?

James Paris Lee (1831–1904)

James Paris Lee was born in Hawick, Scotland in August 1831. In 1836 his family emigrated to Canada where he grew up and developed an interest in firearms. After serving an apprenticeship in his father's clock- and watch-making business he moved to Ontario where he set up on his own account in 1850. While there he married Caroline Chrysler (an early relative of the now-famous car manufacturer). In 1860, with the addition of two sons, Lee moved with his family to Wisconsin in America. Here he experimented with a range of his own and some standard weapons, converting the famous Springfield muzzle loader to a breech-loading system in 1861.

Lee persevered with his obsession of creating a repeating weapon and after years of experimentation and carrying out work for two of America's famous weapons companies, Sharp and Remington, his ideas for a bolt-action magazine rifle were taken up by the British War Office. Manufacture of the now internationally famous Lee-Enfield Rifle commenced at the Royal Small Arms Factory, Enfield Lock in 1895.

James Paris Lee (1831–1904) seated next to his brother, John, from whose foundry, in Wallaceberg Ontario, the first Lee rifle was said to have been fired.

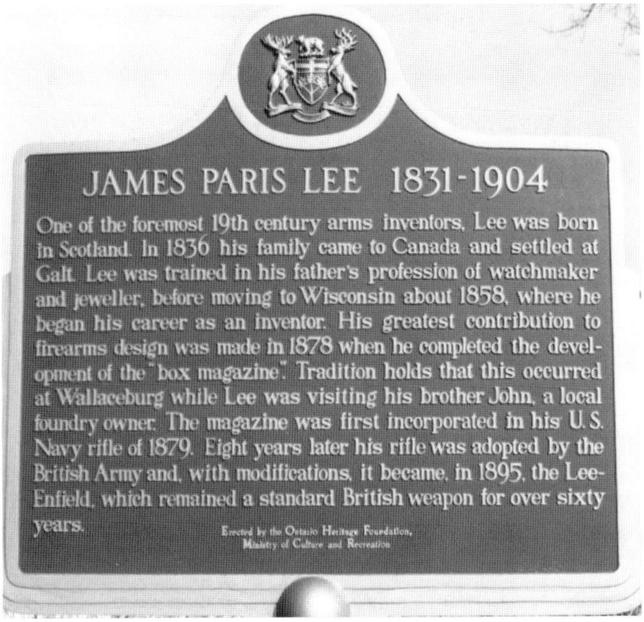

A plaque erected by the Ontario Heritage Foundation, close to the site of the John Lee foundry in Queen Elizabeth Municipal Park, on the north side of the Sydenham River, to commemorate the claim that James Paris Lee fired the first shot from his prototype rifle, in 1879, into an oak plank on the opposite bank.

Amazingly, the later Mk. 4 version of the Lee-Enfield can still be seen in use around the world today. This is not only a lasting tribute to Lee, but it is an acknowledgement of the engineering skills of the Lea Valley workforce who, over the years, produced this weapon in vast quantities.

REFERENCES

House of Lords Record Office, London, subject: "The Trials of nine descriptions of Breech-loading Rifles accepted for competition in accordance with the terms of the War Office Advertisement of 22/10/66", reference, Reports Commissioners 1886-68, XVI, pp.32-4.

Lewis, James H., "The Development of the Royal Small Arms Factory (Enfield Lock) and its Influence Upon Mass Production Technology and Product Design c.1820-c.1880", unpublished PhD thesis, Middlesex University, December 1996.

Skennerton, Ian D., *The Lee Enfield Story*, published by Ian D. Skennerton, Australia, 1993,

Note 1

The Enfield Pattern 1853 rifle was the first weapon in Britain to be made under the mass-production system using interchangeable parts.

Note 2

By 1856 the War Office was responsible for weapon procurement for the armed forces. Formerly this role had been performed by the Board of Ordnance.

5. OVER TWO HUNDRED YEARS OF INNOVATION AT WALTHAM ABBEY

It is probably fair to say that most people do not generally know how the workforce of one small Essex country town helped to change the way our lives are lived today. Without the ongoing research and technical developments that were carried out at what was to become the Royal Gunpowder Mills, and later the Royal Armament Research and Development Establishment (RARDE), our lives might have turned out very differently.

In the twelfth century the town's Abbey was governed by the rules of the Augustinian Order and it is thought that it was the monks who first set up a fulling mill within its precincts, used for the preparation of cloth, and a corn mill, for grinding flour, on channels dug to bring water from the River Lea. Therefore, if this is true, it could be claimed that the monks had inadvertently created the facilities that allowed the later explosives industry to become established at Waltham Abbey, an industry that lasted for over three-hundred years.

About the year 1665 Samuel and Ralph Hudson acquired the mills and converted them for the manufacture of gunpowder. A title deed of 1669 refers to the existence of two powder mills and outhouses for "grindinge, boylinge, corninge and dryinge of powder". By the beginning of the eighteenth century the mills were under the control of the Walton family.

To improve the efficiency of the production process, the celebrated engineer John Smeaton was engaged by William Walton to design new water-powered edge-runner incorporating mills. These were to replace the rather dangerous stamp mills that were operated by a line of workmen, who each had to repeatedly bring down a heavy beam of timber into a bowl of potentially explosive mixture. The job of the workmen was to operate each individual stamp mill until it was judged that the ingredients were suitably crushed and incorporated. Edge-runner, as the name implies, refers to the orientation of the two grindstones that are vertically mounted as opposed to the horizontal mounted stones that are found in corn and other early mills.

Sadly, William Walton did not see all the fruits of his investment in the gunpowder business, as he died intestate in 1711. Philippa, his 35-year-old widow, took over the mills and successfully ran them despite having the added responsibility of caring for her family of ten children.

The Board of Ordnance, a department of government, was the major purchaser of gunpowder for both the Army and Navy. As the eighteenth century progressed, Britain, with her extended empire and deteriorating international relations, needed control of the supply of gunpowder for her armed forces. As demand increased in time of conflict there were further problems in obtaining consistently good-quality powder from the many private manufacturers. A solution to the problems came about when the government purchased the mills at Faversham, Kent in 1759 and, in 1787, those at Waltham Abbey, which were bought from John Walton, the great grandson of Philippa Walton. Philippa had died in 1749 at the age of 74, 38-years after taking over the mills from her late husband.

Lt. General Sir William Congreve (1741–1814) was appointed to purchase the mills at Waltham Abbey on behalf of the British government. In 1787 Congreve bought the mills from John Walton for £10,000.

The man who had been appointed to purchase the mills on behalf of the government was the Deputy Comptroller of the Royal Laboratory at Woolwich, Major, later Lt. General, Sir William Congreve. The sum agreed was £10,000. Congreve was placed in charge of the mills and spent a further £35,000 on buildings and improvements. With Congreve at the helm, Waltham Abbey was about to become a centre of excellence and innovation that would reach forward almost to the millennium. His first task was to set down strict rules for working safely and also for producing powder of uniform quality. This he did by engaging the best of Walton's workmen and also by ensuring that an interchange of knowledge and procedures took place between Waltham Abbey and Faversham.

It was not until 1789, after all the new processes and procedures were

Major General Sir William Congreve (1772–1828) who, in 1814, succeeded his father and was responsible for continuing the modernisation and expansion of Waltham Abbey gunpowder mills. Congreve is probably better known for improving the gunpowder rocket.

firmly in place, that Waltham Abbey produced its first quality powder. To prove the superiority of his powder Congreve set up a trial on Marlborough Downs where ten-inch shells were fired by nine-pound lots of gunpowder taken from different manufacturers, including six in the private sector. The Waltham Abbey powder propelled Congreve's shells over five-hundred yards further than all the others except one (which still fell one hundred and sixty yards short of his greater range of 4,430 yards).

In 1814 Sir William Congreve was succeeded by his son, also William, as second Baronet and Comptroller of the Royal Laboratory at Woolwich. Young William was also given responsibility for the supervision of all the government gunpowder factories – Ballincollig in County Cork had become number three when it was acquired in 1804. William was a talented inventor who had received his technical education at the Royal Academy at Woolwich. In 1791 he was attached to the Royal Laboratory where his father was Comptroller and it was probably these connections that allowed William to carry on in his father's footsteps and continue the programme of expansion and innovation at Waltham Abbey. One of his early improvements came in 1815 when he patented (No. 3937) a superior type of machine to granulate powder once it had been pressed. Some years after it was introduced into production it was reported that the operation of the machine could not be bettered during the period that gunpowder manufacture lasted.

A live firing by the Rocket Troop of the 95th (Rifle) Regiment of Foot of Congreve gunpowder rockets during a re-enactment at the Royal Gunpowder Mills in July 2007.

One of William's most memorable inventions was the improved gunpowder rocket. A crude form of the missile had been used against British troops in India during the late eighteenth century. By the early nineteenth century Congreve, through his experiments, had doubled the range of the rocket to around two-thousand yards and he later set up a factory to manufacture them on West Ham Marsh, adjacent to the River Lea at Bromley-by-Bow. As would be expected, he obtained all his powder for rocket production from the Royal Gunpowder Mills at Waltham Abbey.

Rocket Troop member standing next to Congreve rockets ready for firing. The largest Congreve rocket ever manufactured weighed 32 pounds; the head measured three feet and required a stabilising stick of 15 feet (4.57 metres).

Although not always accurate, sometimes due to the strength and direction of the prevailing wind, the rockets were used with some effect during the Napoleonic campaign at Boulogne, Copenhagen, Leipzig and Waterloo. When such new weapons were introduced to the theatre of war there were reports that their noise, glare and incendiary power caused panic amongst the enemy. Interestingly, Congreve's rockets are famously recorded in the United States national anthem in the verse "the rocket's red glare, the bombs bursting in air". This refers to the conflict with America between June 1812 and December 1814 when the rockets were employed in the bombardment of Fort McHenry.

By the middle of the nineteenth century there was a growing need for an explosive more powerful than gunpowder, as the size of guns increased, through advancements in manufacturing machinery and engineering technology. These improvements in artillery caused

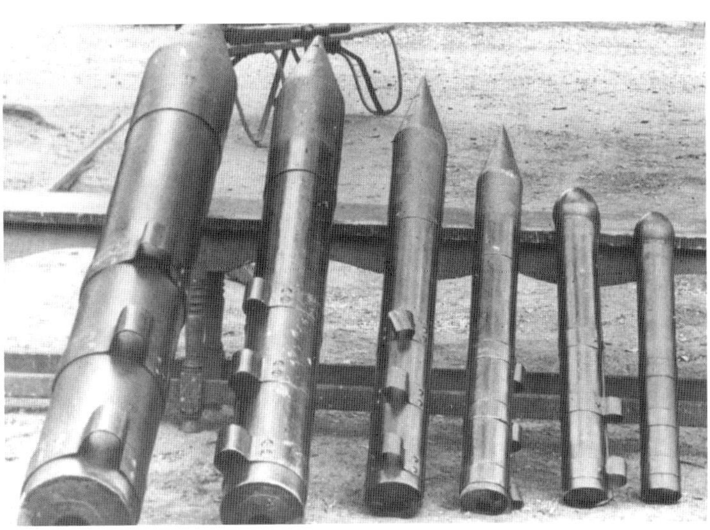

A range of William Congreve's gunpowder rockets.

Sir Frederick Abel (1827–1902) KCB, FRS, was the War Office Chief Chemist. He was responsible for developing the explosive Cordite, which was manufactured in large quantities at Waltham Abbey.

the demise of Congreve's rocket for battlefield purposes but they were adapted as flares (the parachute flare was a Congreve invention) and they were also used for firing safety lines to ships in distress during rescues at sea.

On the Continent, gun cotton (a mixture of nitrating acids on raw cotton) was emerging as the new powerful explosive. Production however was slow and hazardous. In 1863, Sir Frederick Abel, the War Office Chief Chemist set up an experimental plant at Waltham Abbey to test his ideas regarding the safe production of gun cotton. His experiments were successful and the end product proved stable, which gave the ability to manufacture large quantities of the material. Perhaps the greatest compliment to Abel was that his process was widely copied and the product was welcomed not only by the military but also by civil engineers who used it for blasting in quarries and mines.

In 1847 the Italian chemist Ascinao Sobrero, working under T.J. Pelouze at the University of Torino discovered Nitroglycerine, a highly volatile liquid explosive formed by the combination of glycerol and nitric and sulphuric acids. In 1867 the Swedish chemist, Alfred Nobel was able to combine Nitroglycerine with absorbent clay and his invention became Dynamite. In 1890 Sir

Process workers at the Royal Gunpowder Mills in front of a Cordite press. The woman to the left of the picture is holding a length of Cordite, a so-called smokeless explosive. Women workers were taken on at the factory for the first time during the Great War.

Frederick Abel's Explosives Committee, which included the talented chemist Sir James Dewar, devised a new propellant by adding nitrating acids to glycerine and combining the mixture with gun cotton and mineral jelly to form what became known as Cordite. Abel and Dewar patented the invention on behalf of the British government. Apart from devising an explosive that was more stable than some of the earlier materials, it could now be manufactured in long cords by extrusion from a hydraulic press, hence the name Cordite.

Colonel Sir Frederic Nathan (1861–1933), Superintendent of the Royal Gunpowder Mills, Waltham Abbey, 1900–1909.

In the early twentieth century, under the Directorship of Colonel Sir Frederic Nathan, Waltham Abbey saw many improvements in the production of Cordite and gun cotton. Nathan also introduced improvements that were designed to increase efficiency and save money. One of these was a new recovery process for acetone, a solvent used in the manufacture of Cordite. The nitration plant was redesigned for the production of Nitroglycerine and he also introduced new plant for the booster explosive, Tetryl. The improvements and expansion at Waltham Abbey, the only government factory at the time, were, to say the least, opportune, as they allowed large quantities of explosives to be manufactured for the Allies during the First World War.

Apart from the sad human losses and carnage created by war, there is always another inevitable outcome: a rapid increase in technological change brought about as one side strives to gain a major advantage over the other. The First World War saw, for the first time, the coming together of two relatively new technologies, that of the aeroplane and the wireless. The Second World War was to prove no exception to this rule. As each of the belligerents fought for technical supremacy pushing forward the developments in radar, jet engines and explosives at an accelerated rate, an unusual twist to the story took place. The rocket as a weapon of war came back onto the agenda, not quite in the Congreve format as used against military targets, but in the shape of the V2 rocket programme, this time in a more powerful form to be used against a civilian population. Ironically the development was now by German scientists who were leading the world in this secret research.

Sir Barnes Wallis (1887–1979) CBE, FRS, RDI, inventor of the "bouncing bomb" used in the famous raid by the Dambusters (617 Squadron).

As the war continued, the attention of the Allies turned to the vast German manufacturing capability, particularly in the area of the Ruhr Valley that was keeping their military supplied. In Britain, a bold plan was hatched to destroy the Ruhr industries by destroying their source of power. The idea was to breach the three major dams Mohne, Sorpe and Eder to flood the area, which would also deny manufacturers the use of valuable water and reduce the production of electricity. The British inventor Barnes Wallis, then working for Vickers-Armstrong at Brooklands, Surrey, came up with the idea of a bouncing bomb, which he calculated would cause a breach in a dam if dropped at a precise height and distance from a dam wall by an aircraft travelling at the correct speed.

An Avro Lancaster of 617 Squadron that has been specially adapted to deliver the "bouncing bomb" invented by Barnes Wallis.

An early version of Barnes Wallis's "bouncing bomb", round in shape and dimpled like a golf ball.

The first experiments used sphere-shaped bombs dimpled like golf balls but eventually a shape similar to that of a large oil drum was most successful. To ensure a maximum breach, Wallis realised that the bomb would have to sink below the water to a required depth when it met the dam wall, after bouncing across the surface of the reservoir and thus also avoiding the German torpedo nets (the nets had been placed a little distance in front of the wall to prevent underwater missile attacks). Using electric motors to apply backward spin to the bomb before it left the aircraft solved the problem. On the night of 16th–17th May 1943, nineteen specially adapted Avro Lancaster bombers of 617 Squadron, later to become known as the Dambusters, set out from RAF Scampton in Lincolnshire and, despite heavy losses of aircrew and aircraft, achieved their objective.

The final shape of the Barnes Wallis "bouncing bomb" that was dropped on the dams in Germany's Ruhr Valley in May 1943. The dams supplied water and were also a source of electrical power for German industry.

Interestingly the explosive material, a mixture of TNT (Trinitrotoluene) and aluminium, used in each of the bouncing bombs was known as RDX (Research Department composition X). The material's discovery began in Germany in 1899 and was further developed by the German scientist Hertz in the early1920s. After initial investigation of the explosive at Woolwich, new production facilities were set up at Waltham Abbey and manufacture began in early 1939. So in a somewhat ironic way the work that had begun in Britain with Congreve's gunpowder rocket had been taken over and developed beyond recognition in Germany and then used against the British; while the German developed RDX explosive had been manufactured in Britain and used against the enemy in the Dambusters raid.

On 28th July 1945 the Royal Gunpowder Mills closed and on 30th July it reopened as an experimental wing of the government Armament Research Department.This was a major change in status for Waltham Abbey as the site moved from what was effectively a manufacturing facility to one that would become a world leader in experimental science, not just in explosives, but in advanced chemical engineering and rocket propellants. Much of this work was carried out on the facilities that had been established on the south side of Waltham Abbey and known to the workforce as the south site (the original gunpowder mill complex was known as the north site). To achieve the new objectives, graduate engineers, scientists and chemists were recruited and they soon became established as a highly regarded scientific development team. By October 1946, Waltham Abbey had become the Chemical Research and Development Department and would play a major role in designing and experimenting with a range of new materials that would, in the longer term, have a considerable spin-off for not just the military, but also for industrial and domestic markets.

The wartime rocket attacks on Britain and the development of fighter aircraft equipped with jet engines meant that methods of warfare and defence would never be the same again and strategies would have to change dramatically. It was no coincidence that Waltham Abbey was now placed at the forefront of the new emerging technological challenge. For most people this was an anxious period when the world held its breath as it entered a sensitive and critical phase in history. A phase that would become known as the Cold War, which in turn was to provoke an arms race between East and West.

As the Western world's relations with the East became increasingly strained, the emerging technology of the rocket, as a new form of

A Skylark rocket on its launcher. Considerable development of the rocket and its propellant took place at Waltham Abbey, which culminated in the first successful launch from Woomera, Australia in February 1957.

An engineer of the Space Physics Group, Leicester University, preparing the Skylark payload.

Engineers of the Space Physics Group checking a Skylark rocket in the laboratory at Leicester University circa 1967.

A recovered instrument section of a Skylark rocket from the Australian desert.

defence and attack, was being developed by both camps. Interestingly these developments were being ably assisted by scientists who were either taken or had gone voluntarily to countries like Britain, the U.S.S.R. and America and had previously worked within the German V2 missile programme. The push for technological supremacy seemed to begin in earnest with the successful launch, in October 1957, of Sputnik by the Soviet Union, the first artificial satellite to orbit the Earth. This was followed a month later, again by the Soviets, when a live dog was carried into orbit. Naturally, much publicity was given to these events and almost four months later America was forced to respond with the launch of Explorer One, its first satellite. It is probably fair to say that what has become known as the 'Space Race' had begun in earnest.

In the meantime at government establishments in Britain like Farnborough in Hampshire, Wescott in Buckinghamshire and Waltham Abbey in Essex, things had not stood still. Although not as dramatic as the Soviet and American satellite launches, Waltham

Range 'E' at Woomera, Australia. In the foreground can be seen the Skylark launcher and test shops. Lake Koolymilka is in the background.

Ejecting from a jet aircraft cockpit. The ejector seats manufactured by the Martin Baker Company, using propellants developed at Waltham Abbey, have saved the lives of countless airmen.

Abbey scientists, along with their sister establishments had quietly developed the Skylark rocket that was first successfully launched from the rocket range at Woomera, Australia in February 1957. The Skylark had been designed to carry out a range of scientific experiments in the upper atmosphere to understand the significance of such phenomena as ultraviolet, X-ray, gamma and infrared radiation. A greater knowledge of these subjects helped pave the way for the exploration of space.

The power cartridges used for the Sky Flash missile launcher on the Tornado aircraft were developed at PERME, Waltham Abbey.

As technological requirements of the military changed, work on liquid rocket propellants transferred to the Rocket Propulsion Establishment (RPE) at Wescott, and Waltham Abbey began work on new composite propellants and materials, which included those for safely blasting ejector seats from aircraft. In 1973 Waltham Abbey and Wescott were merged, followed, in 1977, with further structural changes, as Waltham Abbey became the Propellants, Explosives and Rocket Motor

Establishment (PERME). This new set-up continued until 1984 when the government decided to privatise the Royal Ordnance factories and Waltham Abbey became divided between the old north site and the south site then became Royal Ordnance plc.

Although the government stopped funding the Skylark programme in 1977, believing that the American Space Shuttle would carry out future research, there was still a future for the project. Skylark was taken over by British Aerospace and later by Matra Marconi Space and became one of the most successful long-term rocket programmes in history, lasting almost fifty years. The final launch, its 441st, under the auspices of the European Space Agency, took place from Sweden in May 2005.

Waltham Abbey was also at the forefront of other research developing a range of propellants for ship-to-air missiles and those used in the mine-clearance system 'Giant Viper', successfully employed in Campaign Desert Storm during the Gulf War. Another highly secret area of research was the investigation of 'Whiskers' technology. This resulted in the development of new fibre-enhanced metals of exceptional strength and durability that are now used extensively by the aerospace and other industries.

In 1991, the Waltham Abbey north site, owned by the Ministry of Defence (MOD), was decommissioned. The south site, as previously mentioned, had already been privatised in 1984. Visitors to the Lee Valley Park today can now enjoy a picnic or a leisurely stroll across

Developed by the Lee Valley Regional Park Authority, the new Country Park, the Gunpowder Park, occupies what was once the "south site" of the Waltham Abbey Royal Gunpowder Mills.

the ground that once formed part of the south site and is now named Gunpowder Park, a new country park.

After a massive decontamination and rebuilding programme, the Waltham Abbey Gunpowder Mills (the north site) reopened as a visitor attraction in May 2001. The Mills still retain much of their unique dual-level canal system that was once used to transport dangerous materials around the site. Also onsite there are in excess of 300 different structures of which English Heritage have listed over 20.

The attractive entrance to the Royal Gunpowder Mills Visitor Exhibition Centre and the "Ignite your Imagination" theatre built on the former "north site" at Waltham Abbey.

It should not be forgotten that the success of the Skylark and the many other research programmes was the result of investigations carried out by that early team of talented scientists and engineers at Waltham Abbey and her sister establishments. The peacetime developments and products that came from these early experiments have changed the way we live our lives today. Imagine a world where we could not undertake major civil-engineering projects such as the building of roads, bridges, tunnels, canals, docks and reservoirs, to create the infrastructure required to help sustain an ever-increasing population. Some of these large-scale projects, including the materials extracted by quarrying and mining, would not be possible without the use of stable explosives. Waltham Abbey scientists and engineers were also responsible for investigating and developing new materials that are currently used in a range of everyday products from protective clothing to some that are used in medical procedures.

Visitors to the site can gain knowledge and also experience the significance of a number of these developments through the various displays that have been designed to inform and excite. These are housed in the recently created exhibition building and also in some of the other restored buildings around the site. Visitors can also enjoy, either by walking at leisure or riding on the Gunpowder Mill's land train, the seventy-one hectares that has been designated a Site of Special Scientific Interest (SSSI) by English

Nature, with the largest heronry in Essex and some of the largest flocks of siskin (a small yellow-green bird not too dissimilar to a greenfinch) in the UK. There is also the opportunity for the visitors to explore and discover for themselves the profusion of wildlife that lives within the thickly wooded areas where at least two species of deer roam free. Afterwards, perhaps over a cup of tea and a scone in the onsite café, the visitor might like to ponder the question, how did the manufacture and development of a range of explosive materials create such a natural haven for so much wildlife?

REFERENCES

Author unknown, "Explosives - OHMS Bicentenary", booklet to commemorate 200 years (1787–1987) of Government ownership of the Royal Gunpowder Mills (Waltham Abbey).

Congreve, William, *The Details of the Rocket System*, London, 1814.

Cooper, Roger, *Rocket Man*, Navtech Systems Limited, Sulby, 2006.

Knapp, Trevor, (Chairman of the Royal Gunpowder Mills Trustees), Interview July 2007.

Lewis, Jim, "The Lea Valley and Britain's Forgotten Greatness", *Electrotechnology*, December 1997/January 1998.

National Archive, Kew: WO1/1120, WO1/1123.

Page, William (ed.), *The Victoria History of the County of Essex*, Vol. 2.

Note 1

The Royal Gunpowder Mills is open as an attraction between April and September and potential visitors should either telephone (01992 707370) or check the website www.royalgunpowdermills.com for further details.

Note 2

Skylark and other rockets like Skura and Petrel were called Sounding Rockets as they 'sounded' the upper atmosphere rather like the term sounding the ocean's depths.

Note 3

The author should like to take the opportunity to thank Roger Cooper of Navtech Systems Limited for generously providing photographs and also for giving advice regarding the Skylark programme. Roger was Senior Experimental Officer with the University of Leicester Space Research Group, and while working as a "Rocket Man" for fifteen years was attached to the British National Space Programme.

6. FROM GUNPOWDER TO TOURISM – THE PEACEFUL EXPLOSION

The Royal Gunpowder Mills at Waltham Abbey, which occupy some 190 acres towards the northern end of the Lea Valley, were in continuous government use from 1787 to 1991. Before this, gunpowder had been produced on the site by the Walton family and before them by the Hudsons. Until steam was introduced in the 1850s, water from the River Lea powered the machinery and charged the site's dual-level canal system. In the twentieth century, the development and manufacture of a range of chemical propellants and explosives, particularly Tetryl and RDX (used in the "Dambusters" raid) helped the Allied Forces win two world wars. The site, now decommissioned, contains over 300 structures, over 20 of which are listed.

The experimental, development and production work carried out at Waltham Abbey has, over the centuries, provided employment and brought economic and social prosperity to the area. Neither was this work for entirely military purposes. The peaceful use of explosives in civil engineering has speeded the construction of roads, bridges, railways, canals and harbours and made the extraction of essential raw materials considerably easier in the mining and quarrying industries. Due to the quality of Waltham Abbey's products, which were recognised internationally, new export markets were opened up to Britain.

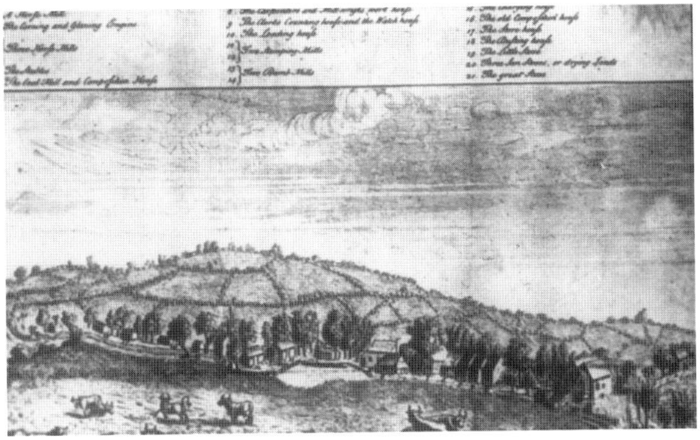

J. Farmer's engraving (1735) of John Walton's Gunpowder Mills at Waltham Abbey, Essex.

In the centre of the picture is a gunpowder barge resting in a dried-up canal. On the right is a protective blast wall. Picture taken autumn 1996.

With the closure of the Mills, economic hardship came to the locality.The question then had to be addressed as to whether any commercial alternatives could be put in place. Solutions to such problems often depend upon a site's particular heritage and accessibility to transport. If a stricken industry or place of manufacture has an interesting historic past, then there is the possibility of developing a long-term strategy based on aspects of that heritage.

Waltham Abbey for many reasons is truly a jewel in the tourism and heritage crown, the site being recognised by English Heritage as "the most important to the history of explosives manufacture in Europe".While the Royal Commission on the Historical Monuments of England (RCHME) has written that the Gunpowder Mills are "the most complex industrial site yet surveyed by the commission". There are also at least thirty-eight A4 pages of references to individual historical documents on the Waltham Abbey Mills located at the National Archive, Kew. As those who seriously study history will know, such a wealth of quality documented evidence is extremely rare.

Because the site had remained in government hands for so long (over two hundred years) and because of the highly secret nature of the work, the place took on the mantle of a forbidden

Powder barges on the dual-level canal system at the Royal Gunpowder Mills at Waltham Abbey. These barges were used for transporting explosive material around the site and not for shipping gunpowder, via the River Lea, to the powder magazines located along the River Thames and elsewhere.

Archaeologists recording details of a powder barge during excavation work at the Royal Gunpowder Mills at Waltham Abbey, circa 1996.

city. External contractors for repair and maintenance were seldom used, the work being carried out internally by a highly skilled workforce who had to comply with the rigours of the Official Secrets Act. These were major factors in the conservation of the site which have clearly helped to guard the integrity of the artefacts.

When a particular source of power for the site's machinery became obsolete, or outlived its useful life, it was replaced with the latest technology. The abandoned technology was then discarded and allowed to fall slowly into a state of decay. This has provided a unique opportunity to trace, study and record the technological changes to the energy sources which drove the various pieces of processing plant, from water through steam to electricity. Apart

Remains of mid-nineteenth-century water-powered gunpowder press house on the site of the Royal Gunpowder Mills, Waltham Abbey, Essex.

from the obvious educational and academic benefits to be derived from such work, much can be learned from studying the past and making comparisons with evolving present-day industrial and technological developments. By a careful analysis of the results, it is often possible to learn important lessons, thus avoiding the repetition of costly mistakes.

The northern end of the Gunpowder Mills site has been designated a Site of Special Scientific Interest (SSSI) by English Nature. Planted in the seventeenth century with alder trees to provide charcoal for the production of gunpowder, the wood now supports the largest heronry in Essex and one of the biggest flocks of siskin (a small yellow-green bird, not unlike the greenfinch) in the UK. In seclusion, and protected by the dense vegetation, live a variety of mammals such as deer, foxes and otters. Here, by man's deliberate interference with nature, we have been accidentally provided with a priceless environmental asset over two hundred years later which as tourists we can all enjoy.

After an extensive programme of decontamination, with the cost of £16 million being met by the Ministry of Defence, a Charitable Trust has been formed to own, conserve and manage the Gunpowder Mills for the benefit of the public. A further role for the Trust is to formulate a strategy for the creation of a large visitor attraction. This will be done by exploiting the site's heritage through the promotion of a plan which will interpret the various processes used in the manufacture of gunpowder. This initiative is well under way, boosted by a grant (in 1997) of £6.5 million from the Heritage

Listed incorporating mills at the Royal Gunpowder Mills, Waltham Abbey, Essex. Picture taken in autumn 1996.

Bridge over a section of the dual-level canal system at the Royal Gunpowder Mills, Waltham Abbey, Essex, with barge quay on the left.

Lottery Fund. Since the opening of the site to the public, several new displays have been set up within the listed buildings including one on small arms and also a firework exhibition. During the summer months several events take place, including themed weekends and re-enactments by specialist groups. These have become increasingly popular as family outings.

While the change of emphasis from manufacturing to tourism will not necessarily bring instant economic benefit for the region, there is the hope that in the longer term the sensitive restoration of many treasured sites within the Lea Valley will create a focus of attention which will encourage new job-creating industries back to the area. After all, we have the model of Ironbridge Gorge and Coalbrookdale, where the unique industrial heritage of the region helped secure considerable manufacturing investment, particularly from abroad, in the nearby town of Telford.

REFERENCES

Bone, Daniel, "The Royal Gunpowder Mills", publicity brochure, Civix, London, September 1992.

Lewis, Jim, "The Lea Valley and Britain's Forgotten Greatness", *Electrotechnology*, December 1977/January 1978.

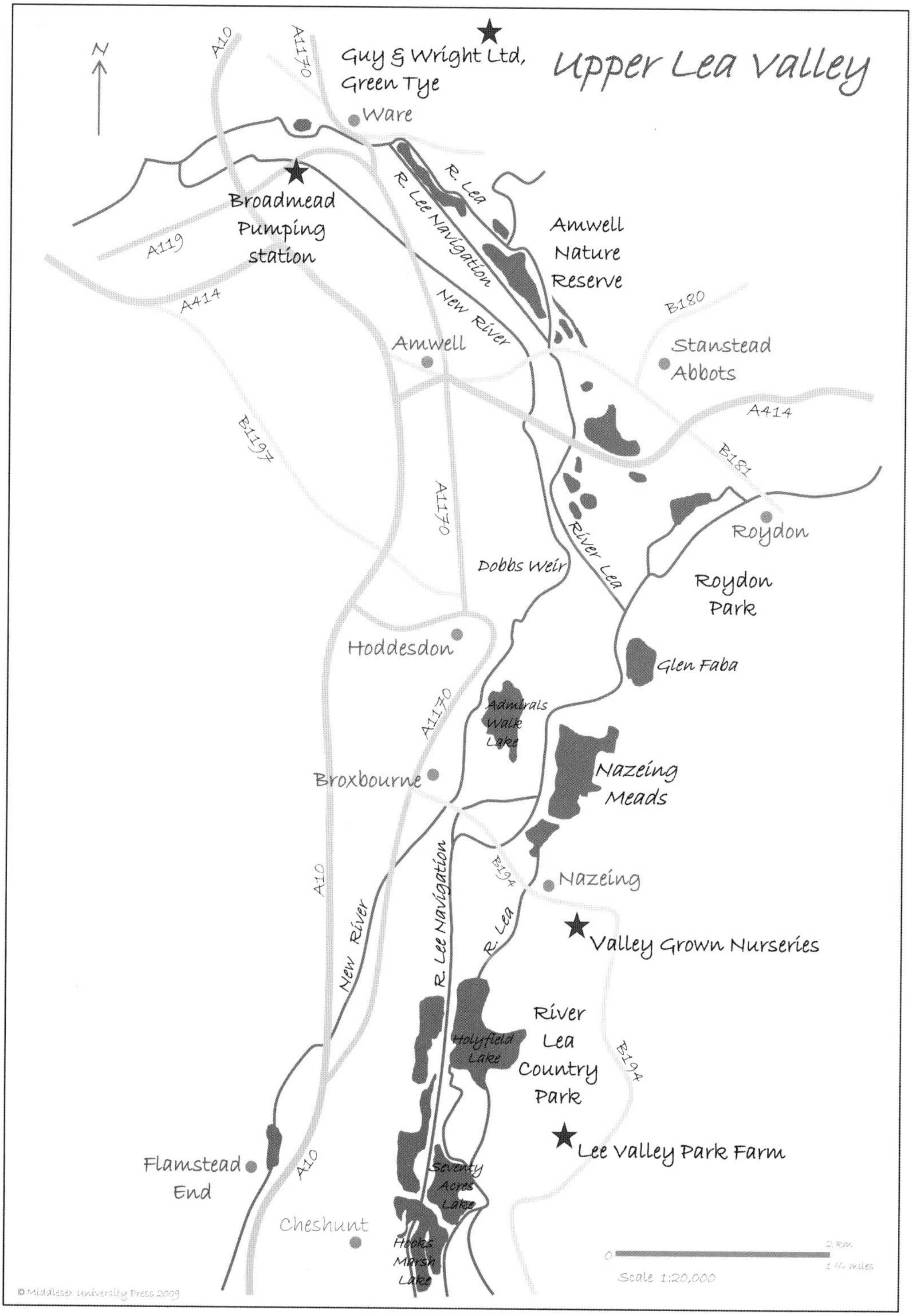
Upper Lea Valley
N
Guy & Wright Ltd, Green Tye
Ware
A10
A1170
A119
A414
R. Lea
R. Lee Navigation
Broadmead Pumping station
Amwell Nature Reserve
New River
B180
Amwell
Stanstead Abbots
A414
B1197
B181
A1170
Roydon
River Lea
Dobbs Weir
Roydon Park
Hoddesdon
Glen Faba
A1170
Admirals Walk Lake
Nazeing Meads
Broxbourne
R. Lee Navigation
B194
Nazeing
A10
New River
R. Lea
Valley Grown Nurseries
River Lea Country Park
Holyfield Lake
B194
Lee Valley Park Farm
Flamstead End
A10
Seventy Acres Lake
Cheshunt
Hooks Marsh Lake
0
2 km
1 ¼ miles
Scale 1:20,000
© Middlesex University Press 2009

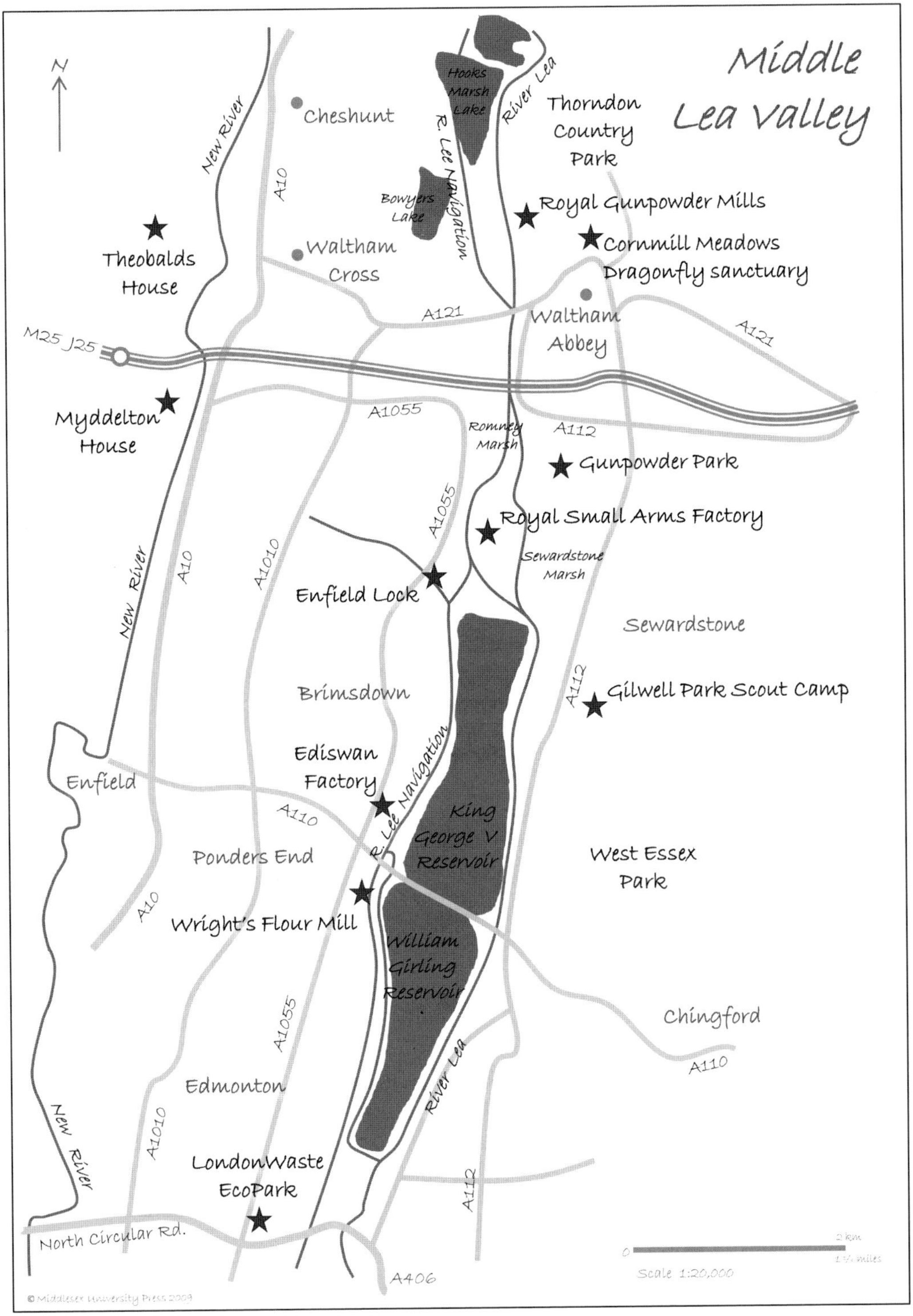
Middle Lea Valley
N
Cheshunt
Hooks Marsh Lake
River Lea
Thorndon Country Park
New River
R. Lee Navigation
A10
Bowyers Lake
Royal Gunpowder Mills
Theobalds House
Waltham Cross
Cornmill Meadows Dragonfly sanctuary
A121
Waltham Abbey
A121
M25 J25
Myddelton House
A1055
Romney Marsh
A112
Gunpowder Park
A1055
Royal Small Arms Factory
Sewardstone Marsh
New River
A10
A1010
Enfield Lock
Sewardstone
A112
Brimsdown
Gilwell Park Scout Camp
Ediswan Factory
R. Lee Navigation
Enfield
A110
King George V Reservoir
Ponders End
West Essex Park
A10
Wright's Flour Mill
William Girling Reservoir
A1055
Chingford
River Lea
A110
Edmonton
New River
A1010
LondonWaste EcoPark
A112
North Circular Rd.
A406
0
Scale 1:20,000
© Middlesex University Press 2009

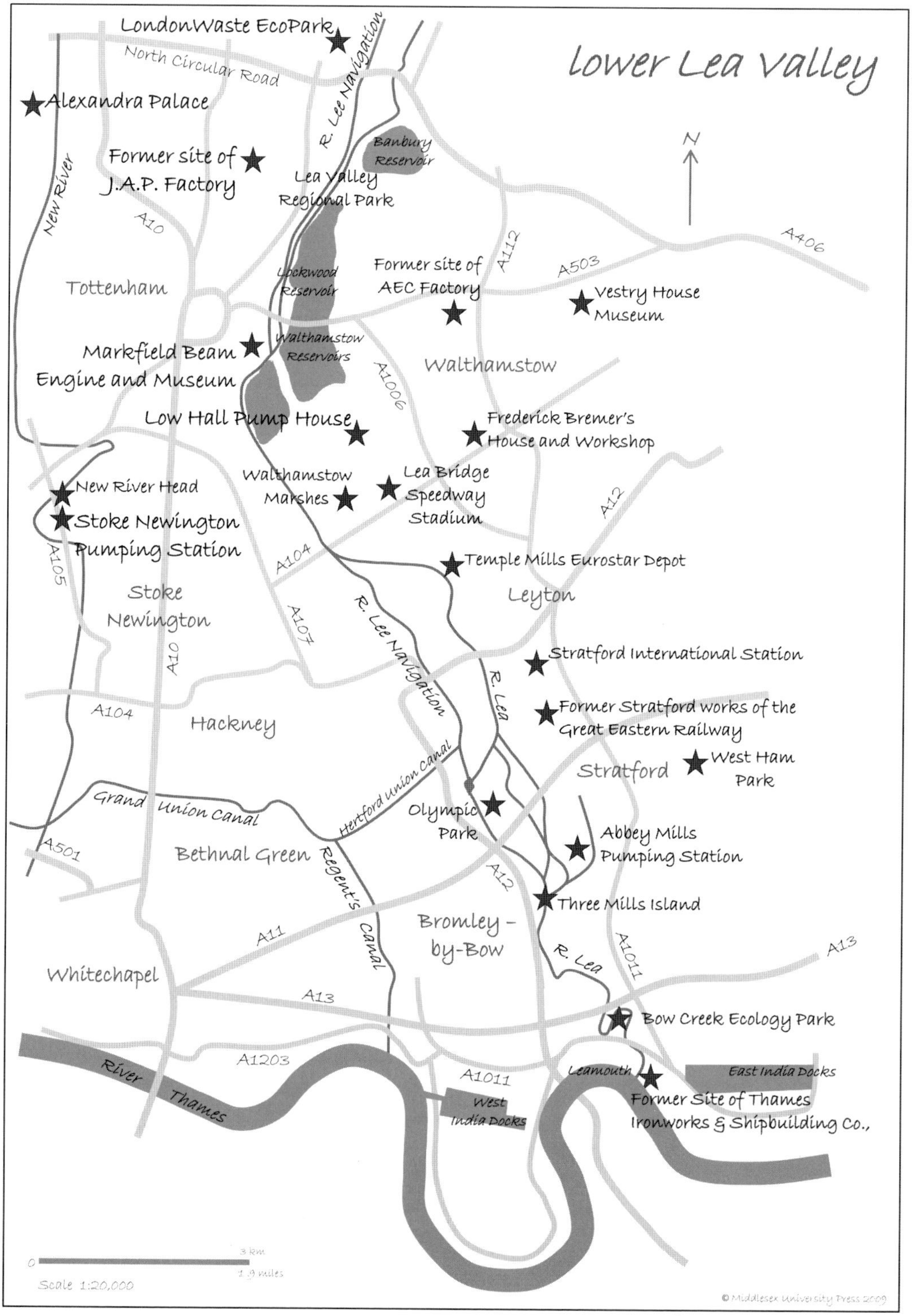
lower Lea valley
N
LondonWaste EcoPark
North Circular Road
R. Lee Navigation
Alexandra Palace
Banbury Reservoir
Former site of J.A.P. Factory
Lea Valley Regional Park
New River
A10
A406
A503
A112
Tottenham
Lockwood Reservoir
Former site of AEC Factory
Vestry House Museum
Markfield Beam Engine and Museum
Walthamstow Reservoirs
Walthamstow
A1006
Low Hall Pump House
Frederick Bremer's House and Workshop
New River Head
Walthamstow Marshes
Lea Bridge Speedway Stadium
A12
Stoke Newington Pumping Station
A105
A104
Temple Mills Eurostar Depot
Stoke Newington
Leyton
A107
R. Lee Navigation
A10
Stratford International Station
R. Lea
Former Stratford works of the Great Eastern Railway
A104
Hackney
Hertford Union Canal
Stratford
West Ham Park
Grand Union Canal
Olympic Park
A501
Bethnal Green
Regent's Canal
Abbey Mills Pumping Station
A12
Three Mills Island
A11
Bromley-by-Bow
R. Lea
A1011
A13
Whitechapel
A13
Bow Creek Ecology Park
A1203
Leamouth
East India Docks
River Thames
A1011
West India Docks
Former Site of Thames Ironworks & Shipbuilding Co.,
0
3 km
1.9 miles
Scale 1:20,000
© Middlesex University Press 2009